CHASING GHOSTS

The Remarkable Story
of One Man's Investigation
of the Assassination
of President John F. Kennedy

by Jim Koepke

PUBLISH
AMERICA

PublishAmerica
Baltimore

First printing

ISBN: 1-4137-1396-3
PUBLISHED BY PUBLISHAMERICA, LLLP
www.publishamerica.com
Baltimore

Printed in the United States of America

Dedicated to Mary, Julie, Jack and the American people.

PublishAmerica books also by Jim Koepke:

Adventures in a Mental Health Center (2002)

CONTENTS

TIMELINE

1961 – Bay of Pigs

November 22, 1963 – Assassination of President Kennedy

1964 – Release of Warren Commission Report

1972 – Watergate Break-in

1976 – House Select Committee on Assassinations Established

1992 – Assassination Records Review Board Is Commissioned

FOREWORD

"Are you writing a book?" That is easily the most frequently asked question I encountered while researching the Kennedy assassination. The first time I heard the question, I was surprised. It had never occurred to me to write a book. I was interested in so many things – the history of the assassination, learning about the different people and events in Dallas on November 22, 1963 – but a book? No, I had no interest in writing a book.

It didn't take long before I was not only unsurprised by the question, I expected it. I suppose that so many people had written books on this subject that it was assumed anyone interested was going to write a book. No, at the time, I had no intention of writing a book, and that was never the reason for my research.

Yet, ten years after I began my research I have, indeed, finally written a book, because the story of my research is so incredible it has to be told. I have to admit that what makes my story so amazing is that it happened to me – an average citizen just like you, with a job, a home in the suburbs, and a family. I wasn't a witness to the events in Dallas, November 22, 1963. I was 9 years old and in the 4th grade in a small town on the Iron Range in Minnesota. My teacher, Mrs. Storbeck, walked into our class and bravely told us that something terrible had happened to President Kennedy. I had no special knowledge of the events, no contacts, no inside information; just an interest in taking the first steps to learning about an important event in America's history.

Over the years, since I took those first steps, I kept thinking about the knowledge I gained from my investigation and how it enlightened my view of this country, the world, and how things happen. The more knowledge one has, the better off he or she is – that much is certain. I decided to share the story of my research into the Kennedy assassination and, in so doing, encourage the people who read this book to think a little about how things in this country work. When you hear something on the news or read an article in the paper, think about whether those who wrote or furnished the story have anything to gain from the perspective that is presented.

PREFACE

On November 22, 1963, President John F. Kennedy was assassinated at age 46, while riding in a motorcade in Dallas, Texas. Beside him in the back seat of his open limousine was the First Lady, Jacqueline Kennedy. Riding in the front seat were Texas Governor Connally, who was injured, and Mrs. Connally. Lee Harvey Oswald was arrested for the shootings, and then two days later, was suddenly killed while in the custody of the Dallas Police, by Jack Ruby.

President Johnson appointed a commission to investigate the assassination, led by Chief Justice Earl Warren. After 10 months of investigation, the commission issued findings that Oswald was the lone gunman, despite eyewitness reports and forensic evidence that contradicted this conclusion.

The American public has long believed in the conspiracy theory. Although a special committee of the U.S. House of Representatives reopened the investigation in 1976, with findings that a conspiracy was likely, government officials and agency spokesmen have continued to dismiss this possibility.

Oliver Stone's 1991 film *JFK* renewed interest and triggered Congress to create the Assassination Records Review Board (ARRB). Led by Judge John Tunheim, the board collected and reviewed the most evidence yet in the 30 years since the assassination. Even so, there is so much more that is unexplained and undiscovered...

CHAPTER ONE:
Getting Started

I was on the phone with Richard Helms, former Director of the Central Intelligence Agency. I fought to control my emotions as he stated that a conspiracy was involved with the assassination of President John F. Kennedy. Mr. Helms concluded our conversation by threatening me. I thought back to eighteen months ago, when I began my investigation into the assassination of President Kennedy. I tried to remember how I had gotten so involved with such a terrible incident. How had an average man arrived at the point where a former Director of the CIA was threatening him?

Eighteen months earlier, I was in search of a hobby. Something to interest me, something to stretch my brain a little bit. This pastime turned out to be the most interesting thing I had ever done, but it had taken a very dark turn. The ride started fast, and now it seemed to be speeding out of control.

I had a demanding job and had come to the conclusion I needed something to do in my spare time at home – an after-work activity that would take my mind off the demands of the clients and staff I worked with. Mundane hobbies had no interest for me. I'm no stamp collector. Researching the death of a president seemed like a challenging and interesting way to spend my time. I didn't realize how deadly it could become.

The reason I began my research into the assassination of President John F. Kennedy is simple – I wanted to know the truth. Whether Lee Harvey Oswald committed the crime or not, whether it was the result of a conspiracy, didn't matter to me in the least. I just wanted to know what happened. The overriding principle I would use throughout my research was the concept of what a "reasonable person" would accept as logical. If anything I studied seemed unreasonable, it could not be accepted by me as credible. As my research progressed, I became convinced that Mr. Kennedy's death was the result of a conspiracy. At that point, the reason for investigating his death changed. Now I did not just want to know the truth, I wanted justice.

Justice, I found, relies on the integrity of our Law Enforcement Agencies. Sadly, I have found neither justice, nor integrity in most of my interactions with these agencies, as you will read.

The impetus to research the Kennedy assassination came from different sources. First of all, I had recently joined the Mensa organization. Mensa encourages its members to conduct independent research groups and facilitates the development of these groups. I recognized that coordinating a Special Interest Group (SIG) would be an effective and interesting way to research a subject. Second, my job as business manager in a local mental health center was very stressful. I needed something distracting to do after hours. Most of all, I wanted something unusual, something that would be different. I needed a project that would hold my interest.

Some time after all the excitement about Oliver Stone's 1991 film, *JFK,* had died down, I decided to see it. I had read a number of articles about it, most of them very negative, and decided to see for myself what it was about. *Newsweek Magazine* (November 22, 1993) had devoted an issue to finding fault with the movie, and their warning about the movie's inaccuracies stayed with me as I went to the theatre. *Newsweek*'s main criticism seemed to be that the movie cut back and forth between real historical footage and re-enactments. The magazine thought this would confuse the average movie-goer. When I brought this up with a friend, his reply was to the point – "How stupid do they think we are?" I agreed. Anyone could see the difference between the movie and the historical footage. Like many people, I learned about events, people, and illegal activities I was unaware of.

Before I watched the movie, I knew as much about the Kennedy assassination as the average citizen – which is to say "probably not much." Once in a while, a news show would feature some researcher who challenged the Warren Commission Report. Usually someone would counter argue and ridicule the research, and so on. This has been a 40-year cycle, with no concrete conclusion.

In 1979, the House of Representatives Select Committee on Assassinations issued a report that concluded there was a conspiracy. Unfortunately, the House report left many leads uncovered and many questions unanswered. The news media reported infighting among the persons involved in the investigation. And of course, the biggest question – why didn't anyone do anything once it was determined there was a conspiracy?

Even a relatively naïve person (such as myself) would be confused about the lack of concern by law enforcement. The House of Representatives stated a president was murdered by a conspiracy, yet law enforcement…doesn't care? Odd indeed. The President at the time was Jimmy Carter, and why he didn't jumpstart an investigation was hard to understand.

So with what little knowledge I had accumulated over the years, I went to the movie, *JFK*, and immediately, became confused. The movie chronicled events that happened at places like Lake Pontchartrain, names of people like David Ferrie and Guy Bannister, all sorts of information that I had never heard about. But I soon learned these people did exist and were key characters in the events of the time.

Several events featured in the movie were so incredible, I questioned at the time whether they were fact or fiction. For example, the movie showed a police officer finding Lee Harvey Oswald (accused of doing all the shooting from the sixth floor of the Texas Book Depository) calmly drinking a soda in the second floor lunchroom moments after the shooting occurred. I reasoned logically that, if true, the Warren Commission would not have been able to satisfactorily resolve this inconsistency. It would certainly have cast grave doubts on Oswald's guilt. Later, I learned this, as was true of the other incredible events portrayed in the film, indeed happened.

I determined that the first and most logical step in my research would be to read the Warren Report. Then I could determine the next steps in my research. In the unlikely event that reading the entire report would show the document's conclusions were reasonable and in order, there would be no need for further research. The Warren Report was poorly written and not an easy read, but included many of the same stories that Stone had in his movie.

The Warren Commission (1963-1964) tried to duplicate the shooting of three bullets with a Mannlicher-Carcano rifle three times within five and a half seconds. They had enormous difficulty accurately duplicating this feat.

The Warren Commission tried to show how Oswald could be drinking a beverage in the lunchroom downstairs right after the shots were fired from the sixth floor of the Depository. The Commission had soldiers run from the sixth floor of the depository and try to make it to the lunchroom (located on the second floor) before someone could run up from the ground floor. No one could duplicate the feat. Of course, this failure should have motivated the Warren Commission to question Oswald's guilt.

One of the constants in the Warren Report is the failure to duplicate or explain key aspects of Oswald's alleged act. Another constant is that it doesn't impact the findings when those same key aspects cannot be duplicated or explained. This, of course, makes no logical sense, and is a violation of the "reasonable person" requirement

Everything the Commission tried to do to prove Oswald was the assassin seemed to do exactly the opposite. What the Warren Commission needed to do, of course, was to follow the evidence to its logical conclusion. The fact that they chose not to do so made one wonder what their purpose really was. I then determined to try the "reasonable person" test. If the Commission wanted to investigate, why didn't they? If the Commission's efforts at duplication failed, what did that mean? The Warren Commission decided to seal the evidence that they had considered, for seventy-five years. If the Commission was so convinced that they proved beyond a reasonable doubt that Oswald was guilty, why seal the evidence for seventy-five years? I had to conclude that the Commission wasn't trying to investigate the crime; rather, it appeared that their sole purpose was to pin the crime on Oswald. They had reached a conclusion, and then were trying to force the evidence to prove their preconceived notion.

Dr. Cyril Wecht, a renowned medical examiner, was allowed to examine some of the sealed evidence in 1969. He discovered that someone had removed what was probably the most important piece of evidence – the President's brain. In this instance, the "sealing" of the evidence by the Warren

Commission facilitated its loss and left the trail cold. Dr. Wecht wrote of his research in his book, *Cause of Death* (1994).

And of course, in the final and most striking failure, the Warren Commission was unable to provide any sort of motive for Oswald to kill the President. How could a prosecutor ever have convinced a jury, beyond a shadow of a doubt, to convict Oswald? I tried to reason that the conclusion of the Warren Report was correct, but to no avail. Time and again, the evidence conflicted with the Warren Commission's conclusions in a way that any reasonable person would question. I couldn't see how anyone could read the Warren Commission Report and agree with their conclusion.

Perhaps the most telling part of the report is near the end, in a section that describes how much Jack Ruby liked dogs. There could be no logical reason for inserting that statement into a report of such national importance. I've sometimes wondered if one of the Commission members inserted this incongruous segment to signal readers that there is something very wrong. It is generally known that at least two members of the Warren Commission disputed the conclusion of the final report. Representative Hale Boggs was reportedly especially adamant in his opposition to the report. Congressman Boggs was killed in 1972 in a plane crash in Alaska. At the time, Mr. Boggs was involved in questioning the possible role of the Nixon Administration in a CIA money laundering scheme in Mexico.

After reading the Warren Report, I decided to review every piece of literature related to the topic that I could. There were very few articles and books written which defended the Commission – small wonder. Unfortunately, most of the books written which were conspiracy oriented were heavy in theory and light in facts. However, I was able to glean through the books, marking off bits and pieces of verifiable information as

I went. Most books about the Kennedy assassination followed the same pattern. The author described some obvious flaws in the Warren Report, then micro-analyzed a small piece of evidence. The author then came up with a theory as to who killed Kennedy. The problem, of course, is that their theory meant nothing – it was somebody's guess. Sure, the author would make a good argument that there was a conspiracy behind the murder of JFK, but they could only guess as to who was responsible.

There were some notable exceptions to the above. Dr. Charles Crenshaw, one of the attending physicians at Parklawn Hospital, wrote a first person account of the assassination, which makes some valid points, and points toward some reasonable conclusions: *JFK – Conspiracy of Silence* (1992). Dr. Crenshaw felt pressured by Lyndon Johnson to get a death bed confession from Oswald, whether Oswald actually confessed or not.

Ret. Col. L. Fletcher Prouty, former Director of Covert Operations for the Joint Chiefs of Staff, used his personal knowledge of intelligence agencies and big business to write a book explaining a likely scenario for how the assassination occurred: *JFK: the CIA, Vietnam, and the Plot to Assassinate John F. Kennedy* (1992). Col. Prouty was active in the military and the intelligence community for many years, including during the tenure of President Kennedy.

Since I wanted to make sure I covered both sides of the assassination question, I made a determined effort to find every book I could that was pro-Warren Commission Report. This was difficult, as there wasn't much written in support of the Warren Report.

One pro-Warren book was by David Belin, who had been a part of the Warren Commission: *Full Disclosure* (1988). I had some real problems with his book. First of all, he had a lot to lose should he, as a participant, later contradict the Warren Commission Report. His name and status depended on the Commission being right. Second, his book seemed, again, less of an investigation and more of an effort to twist every piece of evidence until it could somehow be used to incriminate Oswald. The book reminded me of another country's cold war era's "investigating and documenting methods"; i.e. it was self-serving, and you couldn't believe a word said. Mr. Belin's book did little to inspire confidence in its conclusion supporting the Warren Report.

The most well-known book supporting the Warren Commission was titled *Case Closed*, by Gerald Posner (1994). He was the hero for whom Warren Commission supporters waited thirty years. His work completely supported the Warren Report. The book takes the same tact as the Warren Commission; i.e. Oswald is guilty, now let's figure out how the evidence can be made to support that fact. To me, this slanted approach was the tip-off that all was not well with the book, which relied heavily on name calling. Persons who were not pro-Warren Commission are sometimes called mad, alcoholic, or just untrustworthy. There was no tolerance or respect in this book for any opinion but that of the Warren Commission. Yet the findings in the book do not give credence to Warren Report conclusions.

At this point, I decided not to follow the same procedure that everyone else had. Sure, I could micro-analyze some evidence, then come up with a theory about who had the means, motive and opportunity, but I wanted more. I wanted to know the truth. I spent a lot of time at the library researching the assassination and its aftermath. Over and over I tried to come up with something that someone else had missed.

Finally, it came to me – many people who were in a position

of power during the assassination were still alive. I would contact, by letter, every person still living who could reasonably be expected to have some knowledge of the Kennedy assassination.

The time factor, thirty years having elapsed, could actually be beneficial to me. I reasoned that as people get older, they understand they aren't going to live forever, and may wish to ease a guilty conscience, or set the facts straight. I planned to offer, if desired, to keep all information confidential until after the individual's death.

I considered the possibility of putting out a "call for evidence," a request for people in cities such as Dallas and New Orleans, maybe Miami, Washington D.C., or New York, to come forth with any evidence they may have been holding for thirty years. The best and maybe the only effective way to do this would have been to take out large newspaper ads in several cities. This turned out to be too expensive an undertaking. At about the same time in 1992, a Congressionally funded organization, the Assassination Records Review Board (ARRB), put out a call for evidence. It accumulated a tremendous amount of material – over five million documents. Yet, its success and effectiveness remains to be seen.

I chose the affordable alternative. I made up a list of the persons who had held positions of power in 1963. I promised anonymity to those who required it. Some I promised to keep secret whatever information they gave me until their death.

I knew I had to get some national exposure. I was a member of the Mensa organization. In order to get the word out, and maybe make some contacts, I wrote to Mensa and asked their permission to start a research special interest group (SIG) into the assassination of President John F. Kennedy. Mensa agreed and included the SIG description in their quarterly magazine.

It took less time than I expected for things to happen.

CHAPTER TWO:
Sam's Amazing Revelations

On March 3, 1993, I came home from work and found the quarterly Mensa journal in my mailbox. I thumbed through it and found a listing of all Special Interest Groups (SIGs). My JFK research special interest group (SIG) was listed there for the first time. I expected that over the next few weeks I might get a few letters from persons who had a theory or an idea. It didn't seem reasonable to expect much more than a small lead. Honestly, I didn't know if there was going to be any interest at all. I settled into my usual after-work routine.

Later that evening, I received a call from a person I will refer to here as Sam. Sam spoke with a bit of a drawl. He told me he was a Texan who had relocated to a different part of the country for business purposes.

Sam saw my SIG listing in the Mensa journal and asked me if I had ever heard of Billie Sol Estes. I remembered reading that Estes was an associate of Lyndon Johnson's and had been in trouble with the law. Sam seemed relieved when I told him this. He then proceeded to tell me an incredible story. Of course, I cannot confirm that any of the following is true. I can only share the amazing story he told me.

Sam knew Billie Sol Estes through a mutual friend. Estes gave the mutual friend an audio tape that implicates Lyndon Johnson in the murder of President Kennedy. First, Sam explained the audio tape recorded a conversation that took place at a meeting in 1963. Vice-President Johnson had gathered for a meeting with Allen Dulles (former Director of the CIA and later a member of the Warren Commission) and a representative of Carlos Marcello (a Mafia kingpin).

Estes also attended. He was in trouble with the law and secretly taped the conversation. Estes was fearful of what would happen to him and wanted the tape as insurance for his own welfare.

There were three tiers to the plot – the CIA, Lyndon Johnson, and the Mob. A sub-group to the Mob was the Union, under Jimmy Hoffa. Money was funneled through the Union for this job.

H.L. Hunt (not present at the meeting), then a supporter of Johnson, reportedly gave $10 million to LBJ. Sam wasn't clear if this money was earmarked for the assassination or for Johnson's personal use. Hunt was famous as a wealthy Texas oilman, who allegedly purchased an ad which severely criticized President Kennedy in the Dallas newspaper the day of the assassination. Hunt left Texas and traveled to Mexico in late November because he was concerned that the truth about the assassination and that he financed the principals would be revealed. Much of this same story has been alleged by conspiracy theorists in other writings.

At the meeting, someone asked what would happen if President Kennedy were killed. Johnson replied that there were two parts to the process. The first, he said, was the actual deed. The second was the cover-up, which would have to be controlled by the new president. Johnson told the group, "You do your part, and I'll do mine." Sam was quite clear that Lyndon Johnson had no hand in the plotting or carrying out of the assassination. His sole link would be to guarantee that no real investigation took place and that none of the principals would be punished.

Each of the three tiers contributed a team of shooters and spotters – one in the Texas Book Depository, one in the Dal-Tex building, and one on the grassy knoll. The mob's shooter was Charles Harrelson (who is now serving a life sentence for murdering a Federal judge). Johnson's connection was Malcolm Wallace, a longtime friend of the Vice-President. In the 1990's, it was discovered that one of the hand prints found in the "sniper's nest" (the sixth floor) of the Texas Book Depository right after the assassination matched Malcolm Wallace's. Billie Sol Estes testified before a grand jury that Wallace once murdered someone at Lyndon Johnson's behest. I verified this through research in newspaper articles found at the library: David Hanners's article on p. 4 of the March 23, 1984 *Dallas Morning News*, Billie Sol links LBJ to murder. Put all these pieces together, and the result is frightening.

Something happened to chill the conversation when I asked Sam to name the shooters for the CIA team. He refused to answer my questions. I asked him pointedly if E. Howard Hunt and his Cuban followers were involved, but he would not answer. I didn't want to push Sam, since he was providing some fascinating information, so I let him go on. Sam said that the plan had always been to pin the crime on Oswald. Oswald's quirky personality made him a perfect patsy. Oswald was supposed to leave the Texas Book Depository by a different entrance than he used. The plan was to have a Dallas police officer in place who would shoot and kill Oswald when he walked out the door. Estes guessed that Oswald panicked and fled, or purposely chose a different exit because he knew something was wrong.

Estes didn't know for sure if Oswald shot Officer Tippit; however, "if Oswald didn't shoot Tippit, I don't know who did." It made sense that Oswald killed Tippit, since he had to have been worried about his own safety, given the circumstances.

We spoke for quite a long time. Sam told me repeatedly that the person who had a copy of the audio tape (the mutual friend of Sam and Billie Sol Estes) was quite worried about his own safety. Sam then told me that an informal group, some of whom were involved in the assassination, still controls much of what happens in this country. He said the group's power is based in the CIA, American business, and, to a lesser extent, the Mob.

Sam quoted an example Estes gave him about this powerful group. Estes said that retired Texas Senator John Tower, who had died in a plane crash in 1991, was murdered. Estes said that "Tower was no longer of any use." Sam explained that Senator Tower was aware of countless illegal schemes, from Kennedy's assassination on. Senator Tower's debacle in trying to be President Bush's Secretary of Defense proved his career, and thus his power and usefulness, was over. (Senator Tower was asked by the elder George Bush to be his Secretary of Defense. Tower performed so poorly at the Senate hearing that he did not become the Secretary – furthermore, his public career was ended.) Additionally, it is possible Senator Tower was reflecting on his life's mistakes and was regretful. Tower could not be allowed to confess his, or others', crimes.

The above-mentioned informal group of powerbrokers sought approval for Senator Tower's death from a well-known United States Senator. According to Sam, this group was still in power, so there was still a great deal of danger to anyone who may expose the truth.

As a further example of this group's power, Sam then told me a story about a retired Texas Ranger, U.S. Marshall Clint Peoples. Peoples had investigated Estes for his connection to a murder that Lyndon Johnson had ordered in the 1960's. Estes testified before a grand jury in 1984 and implicated President Johnson in the murder. Then, at the grand jury investigation, Estes was asked about Johnson's involvement in the Kennedy assassination. Estes refused to answer. (Reported by William P. Barrett and Charlotte-Anne Lucas in the Sunday, March 24, 1984 *Dallas Times Herald* article, "Sources: Estes wouldn't testify on JFK assassination.")

U.S. Marshall Peoples then decided to investigate the Kennedy assassination, using Estes as his source. The same group of people who had Senator Tower killed had U.S. Marshall Peoples killed. He was killed in a one-car accident (1992). The official story was that Peoples' death was accidental.

As this 45-minute phone call wound down, I asked Sam for his phone number. He was a bit reluctant to give it to me, but said, "Well, I guess it won't hurt anything." I later called him back, and he confirmed everything he told me in our initial conversation.

It was obvious I had a lot of work to do. I understood that there were many people who made up stories about the Kennedy assassination. Some hoped to make money, some sought fame, and some were just plain nuts. Sam did not strike me as any of those. He was very calm, very collected, did not ask for money, and the last thing he wanted was fame. Had I not asked him for his phone number, I would have never been able to contact him. Was Sam telling the truth?

The story he told me was too involved and detailed to have been made up just for me. After all, the Mensa journal with my name and SIG description had just come out. Also, my phone number wasn't listed. He must have wanted to talk to me enough to go to the trouble of finding me. Some of what Sam told me was standard fare. Charles Harrelson's name had been mentioned before in connection with the Kennedy assassination.

Billie Sol Estes was featured in newspaper articles in the *Dallas Morning News* and *Dallas Times Herald* (previously cited), several years ago when he testified before a grand jury about Lyndon Johnson. The idea of an informal group of business, political and CIA agents controlling certain aspects of the country is a subject that Ret. Col. L. Fletcher Prouty has written about in his 1992 book, *JFK: the CIA, Vietnam, and the Plot to Assassinate John F. Kennedy.*

Anyone who is familiar with Billie Sol Estes will have heard his name mentioned as someone who is on the "shady" side. At times, law enforcement associates with shady characters when investigating a crime. Apparently, the law enforcement authorities in Texas thought enough of Billie Sol Estes' credibility to have him testify before a grand jury. If the law enforcement system thought that Billie Sol Estes possessed enough integrity to be a credible witness, then I felt I should pay some heed to what was I being told.

Two major new insights were revealed by Sam. First, the existence of an audio tape, which would prove there was a conspiracy to kill Kennedy and also implicate Lyndon Johnson, the CIA, and the Mob. Second, the linking of Senator John Tower to the assassination, and blaming his death on an ongoing secret power cartel.

The first thing I did was to research Billie Sol Estes, Senator Tower, and U.S. Marshall Clint Peoples. I found everything exactly as Sam had told me.

The grand jury investigation did take place; Estes did implicate Johnson; Peoples did work with Estes; the obituary on Peoples did claim a one-car accident. So far, this was proving very intriguing.

I then researched Senator Tower's plane crash. This subject got interesting very quickly. I went to the library and pulled up the *New York Times* article on the crash. Engine trouble was reported as the probable cause of the crash. This appeared open and shut. Since I wanted to follow-up and confirm everything, I contacted the FAA in what should have been a routine process.

Now it really began to get interesting. The person I contacted at the FAA, in December 1993, pulled up the report on her computer for me. She said that the cause of the crash was "undetermined." I explained to her that the *New York Times* had said the cause of the crash was engine trouble. She said that was not correct, that the cause was "undetermined." I asked her for the name of the investigator who made this report. She checked and said all information regarding that had been removed from the computer files. I asked if that was normal. She said she had never seen it happen before.

Obviously, this made me wonder if what Sam had told me was correct. It did seem quite odd. I decided to file a Freedom of Information Act (FOIA) with the FBI to see if they had done an investigation, in early 1994. Apparently, they had, for they accepted the request. They informed me that it may take two years or more to produce the report, due to the backlog. On November 8, 1996, I received a partial packet of information from the FBI regarding the crash of Senator Tower's plane. The plane crashed while approaching the Glynco (Georgia) airport. The possibility of engine trouble was discussed in the report. I realized the plane was probably landing at the FLETC (Federal Law Enforcement Training Center) facility in Glynco. There will be more about the FLETC facility in Glynco later in this book.

At this point, in early 1994, I began my letter writing campaign. I contacted retired Col. L. Fletcher Prouty, mentioning my questions about the assassination and Senator Tower. Col. Prouty worked closely with Intelligence Operations for many years, was the Special Operations Officer for the Joint Chiefs of Staff in the early 1960's, and also advised President Kennedy. He was quite familiar with the circumstances surrounding the death of President Kennedy, and was the man portrayed in the movie *JFK* by Donald Sutherland.

Col. Prouty responded by letter in March 1994, apparently nonplused about the possibility that Senator Tower might have been murdered. Maybe after all his experience with covert operations throughout his career, nothing surprised him. We corresponded back and forth and developed such a friendly working relationship over the next couple of years that I began to refer to him as he signed his letters, "Fletch." He introduced me to the intelligence community and did much to open my eyes about how things worked. He was a wealth of information about covert operations. The man had "been there and done that" in the world of intelligence. Fletch was a great source of encouragement and sometimes was brutally honest.

I told Fletch about the *New York Times* article about Senator Tower and my encounter with the FAA. He didn't think much about the FAA and thought maybe the *Times* knew more about what happened.

I supposed anything, from a bureaucratic snafu to purposeful destruction of files, could be responsible for the missing data at the FAA. This wasn't the only time I ran up against this type of road block.

CHAPTER THREE:
William Colby

I wrote former CIA Director William Colby a letter regarding the assassination and the possible connection to Senator Tower (1994). Mr. Colby was director of the CIA from 1973 to 1976. He had worked at the CIA almost since its beginning. During his tenure at the CIA, he was responsible for operations in the Vietnam War, including the infamous "Phoenix" program. This counter-insurgency program resulted in over twenty thousand deaths, some of them allegedly civilians. Mr. Colby felt that the Phoenix plan itself was sound, but those in charge on the ground may have greatly misused the power they were given.

When one writes people who have attained his status, one expects no more than a form letter from a secretary, if that. One can only imagine how many letters he has thrown in the wastepaper basket. My guess is that ex-CIA Directors get more such letters than most people. But I knew that if there was any truth to what Sam had told me, my letter might get Colby's attention.

I felt that Mr. Colby was a good choice. First of all, he was removed as Director of the CIA because he cooperated too much with the ongoing Congressional CIA investigation. When asked for specific information by Congressional investigators, he provided it to them. This did not seem to sit too well with President Gerald Ford, or some of his advisors.

Mr. Colby appeared to me to be someone who was a good soldier, but of course, would not submit to any witch hunts. As long as I focused the letter on as few items as possible, I thought there might be a chance he would read it.

Three days after I sent the letter, Mr. Colby phoned me. As surprising as that was, it got even more so. Mr. Colby said that he would tell me the same thing he told Mr. Oliver Stone when he came to talk with him: "If I had any evidence that the CIA was complicit in the assassination of President Kennedy, I would have investigated." This sounded like a standard denial, and who could blame him. I was more interested in the evidence that pointed to conspiracy, especially the Senator Tower connection I had recently learned about. As we discussed the assassination and Senator Tower, Mr. Colby had another surprise for me.

William Colby began to plead his case. I mean that he took on the attitude of "please believe me." This was totally unexpected. I was stunned. Given who he was – a very important man, and who I was – an average Joe, it was incredible! He pleaded with me to believe him!

Mr. Colby told me that he was not denying the possibility of a conspiracy, or the possible involvement of CIA agents. The official CIA structure, of course, he assured me, would never have been involved in the assassination of President Kennedy. I had no quarrel with that statement, as it would have been foolhardy for the agency itself to make the murder of the President a policy statement. Mr. Colby did leave the door open for the possibility of agents employed by the CIA operating outside the agency's policies. He also explained how difficult it would have been to just launch an investigation of the agency without any concrete proof in hand.

Even though he was the Director of the CIA, it would not have been possible, politically or operationally, to conduct such an investigation without solid evidence already in hand. Mr.

Colby stated that he was a lawyer by training, and his training required him to have some concrete evidence before embarking on an investigation as controversial as the Kennedy assassination.

Three times Mr. Colby tried to extricate himself from blame for not conducting an investigation of the Kennedy assassination. "If I had the proof in hand, I would have investigated and gone after those responsible." It seemed to me that Mr. Colby was trying to provide a bit of protection for himself. It's important to keep in mind that, to him – as well as to anyone else in the world – I would be considered just an average citizen.

The manner of Mr. Colby was more than surprising – it was shocking. He was literally pleading with me to believe him. Why in the world would he feel he had to plead his case to me? The only reason I could imagine that he was doing this was because of something I had written in my letter. My letter had two major points of discussion: (1) the issue that CIA operatives were involved in the assassination of President Kennedy, and (2) the issue that Senator John Tower was murdered and that his murder was committed by a covert power cabal (not the least of whose membership was a United States Senator). My letter had dealt with the above issues as possibilities. The more I spoke with Mr. Colby, the more these issues seemed less like possibilities and more like probabilities.

Was it possible there really was a business/political/ intelligence agency cartel that controlled certain events in the United States? Two years later, the news media would report that American business interests had arranged for the CIA to spy on French business. For every such report that made the newspaper, one had to wonder how many others never saw the light of day.

Our conversation was winding down, and I could sense Mr. Colby wanted to say goodbye. I then asked him what route he suggested I follow to further look into these issues.

Mr. Colby made the boldest statement to me that he could possibly make: He told me to "forget all about this, just forget about it." Up to now, his frank, sincere manner had been delivered in a very calm, rational tone of voice. Now, Mr. Colby came across very terse and forcefully. He certainly wanted to make an impression on me that this investigation was something I should not be doing. I did not take this as a personal threat, but rather as more of a "friendly" warning that I was getting too close to something. No one's ever accused me of having too much good sense. I pushed on, asking him if he would take one more question.

I described the circumstances surrounding George de Mohrenschildt's death in 1977, and asked him what he thought about the instance. Mr. de Mohrenschildt was a friend of Lee Harvey Oswald's, who had been linked with wealthy business interests and the CIA. When the House Select Committee on Assassinations conducted its investigation in 1977, one of their staff, Mr. Gaeton Fonzi, went to Florida to question Mr. de Mohrenschildt. (Mr. Fonzi has written a book titled, *The Last Investigation* (1993) that chronicles his part in the House Select Committee on Assassinations.) Mr. Fonzi was unable to question de Mohrenschildt, but left his business card. A short time later, de Mohrenschildt was found dead from a gunshot wound with Mr. Fonzi's card in his shirt pocket. Mr. De Mohrenschildt's death was ruled a suicide.

Mr. Colby paused a moment. I sensed he was wrestling with possible responses. He finally said, "I don't know anything about that." I thanked him and said goodbye.

I have several very strong impressions of my conversation

with Mr. Colby. First, he came across as highly intelligent and clear thinking. Second, he was defensive about his lack of action regarding investigation of the Kennedy assassination while he was the Director of the CIA. Why did he feel he had to plead his case to me? Something in the letter I sent him got his attention. After reading my letter, he called me and made a determined effort to convince me he had no part in covering up evidence for the CIA. He never denied that people who worked for the CIA could have been involved in Kennedy's death. He never denied that there could have been a conspiracy. Mr. Colby was trying to tell me something but, of course, couldn't come right out and discuss that kind of information.

Finally, the Senator Tower incident was definitely on his mind. And of course, the final thing, the warning. What was he warning me about? My impression is that he was not intending to threaten me. I don't think that ever crossed his mind. I do think he was telling me that I may be close to crossing a line which could get me into a lot of trouble with someone. Even though Mr. Colby was no longer the Director of the CIA, I have no doubt that he still had contacts in the intelligence community and that he knew one could easily put oneself into a dangerous situation.

Fletch Prouty seemed more concerned than I was about William Colby. He warned that I had "gotten under [Colby's] skin" and that Colby was "volatile" (appendix, document 4). That may be. Fletch certainly knew Colby better than I did. But I was going to stick with my feelings on this one. I felt William Colby meant me no harm – he was actually trying to be helpful.

I spent some time afterward wondering if Mr. Colby was going to look into the Senator Tower story I discussed with him. At the time, I thought a former CIA Director could do pretty much whatever he wanted. Surely, I thought, no one dared mess with a person of such stature.

I was concerned, to say the least, when I heard of Mr. Colby's death (1996). Although Mr. Colby was an older person, he was supposedly in good health, and the circumstances surrounding his death seemed a bit odd. He had apparently fallen out of his canoe and drowned, probably due to a stroke. There is a story that his dinner was found, uneaten, on the table and his computer was left on. Well, sometimes a person isn't hungry and decides to go for a walk, or, I suppose, a canoe ride. The thing that bothered me about this was Mr. Colby was an experienced canoeist. I've been canoeing myself for about twenty years and find a canoe to be a stable, secure vehicle on the water. Were I to collapse suddenly in my canoe, I don't see how I could fall out of it.

After some time passed, I contacted Mr. Colby's wife by letter. I expressed my condolences and asked some questions about whether her husband had mentioned any interest in Senator Tower. Ms. Colby phoned me and came across as an intelligent, gentle spirit who certainly loved her husband very much. She praised William Colby and cherished her memories of him. She does remember him talking about the death of Senator Tower and that he was interested in the event. Ms. Colby did not remember him saying the Senator's death was not an accident and her integrity was so strong that I certainly believe her.

I felt I was on the right track. I decided to contact more people who might be of help. I continued to correspond with Col. Fletcher Prouty, to get his ideas on my conversation with Mr. Colby and further guidance for my research. Mr. Prouty left no doubt about his beliefs (appendix, document 4).

I also decided to contact the Texas Rangers, to see if they had any information about the death of Clint Peoples. I sent them a letter describing some of the information that Sam had given me, asking if they would be interested in speaking with me.

A Texas Ranger phoned me shortly after sending the letter. He tersely told me that Mr. Peoples died in a one-car accident, "and that's all it was, an accident." It did seem strange that this person did not want to discuss any of the information I said I had. I had thought that this was a pretty tight organization, and that if one of the Rangers might have been murdered, that others in the organization would want to follow up on it.

It seemed appropriate to contact Mr. David Belin, who served on the staff of the Warren Commission and was still one of its most ardent defenders. I wrote Mr. Belin a letter, which was brief and to the point. Mr. Belin returned a letter to me (February 1994) that said he didn't have time to answer my letter, but then attached several pages of documents supporting his view. Mr. Belin's attached materials are a prime example of the disinformation that is rampant from the Warren Commission. The attachments were: A *New York Times* Op-Ed submission by David W. Belin, Saturday March 7, 1992, titled "Earl Warren's Assassins"; and a *New York Times* Op-Ed submission by David W. Belin, Friday June 25, 1993, titled "Connally's Wounds Held No Secrets."

Mr. Belin's Op-Ed articles state that none of the doctors at Parklawn Hospital thought that Governor Connolly's wounds came from the front. But why in the world would he bring that point up? To the best of my knowledge, no one has questioned the direction of Governor Connolly's wounds. Mr. Belin attempts to confuse his audience with misdirection. What matters, of course, is the fact that most of the doctors at Parklawn did believe that the President's throat wound appeared to be an entrance wound. Why does Mr. Belin not mention this? Why focus on the direction of the wounds of Governor Connolly? I could only come up with two reasons. The first reason would be to purposely obfuscate the situation and confuse the reader. The second reason would be that the evidence supporting the Warren Report was so thin that grasping at straws was all one could do.

CHAPTER FOUR:
Richard Helms

Next, I decided to compile my information and contact Richard Helms, the Director of the CIA from 1966 to 1973. Mr. Helms would be knowledgeable of events during two dark periods in this country's history, the Kennedy assassination and Watergate.

The Watergate scandal began June 17, 1972 when five employees of Nixon's re-election campaign broke into the Democratic National Committee's headquarters in the Watergate apartment complex. The five burglars were attempting to bug the telephones and steal political documents to learn the opponent's campaign strategy. The leaders of the group were G. Gordon Liddy (a former FBI agent) and E. Howard Hunt (a former CIA agent, who had helped to plan the failed Bay of Pigs operation). A taping system in the Oval Office had secretly recorded meetings and phone conversations. The scandal and cover-up eventually caused President Nixon to resign as President in 1974.

The Bay of Pigs invasion was an attempt led by the CIA in 1961 (during President Kennedy's term) to overthrow Fidel Castro, a leftist dictator in power since 1959. The three-day operation failed without air support and when the Cuban people did not join forces in the attempt.

My interest in Mr. Helms began with a passage from the book written by Mr. Robert Haldeman, *The Ends of Power*

(1978). Mr. Haldeman was the Chief of Staff to President Nixon. According to Mr. Haldeman, during the Watergate crisis, President Nixon told him to meet with Richard Helms. Nixon told Haldeman to tell Helms to block the FBI investigation of Watergate.

Mr. Nixon, according to the Watergate tapes, was concerned that an investigation would "open a scab" and not do the country or the CIA any good. Mr. Nixon was especially concerned about E. Howard Hunt and his Cuban team. According to the Watergate tapes, Nixon suggested paying off E. Howard Hunt for his silence.

President Nixon told Haldeman that if Helms refused to cooperate, he should say that an investigation by the FBI could open up the "whole Bay of Pigs" thing. Haldeman did exactly as President Nixon told him to. He asked Helms to block the FBI investigation. Helms refused. Haldeman then told Helms that an investigation could open up the whole Bay of Pigs thing. At this remark, Haldeman reported that Helms got very agitated and began shouting that Watergate had nothing to do with the Bay of Pigs. The room was suddenly in chaos.

Haldeman later learned that the term "Bay of Pigs" was a code word for the Kennedy assassination. Nixon, via Haldeman, was telling Helms that the truth about the Kennedy assassination would become public knowledge if there was an investigation into the Watergate burglary, and this would not do the CIA or the country any good. Logically, the truth would hurt the CIA, if the CIA had a hand in President Kennedy's death. It also follows that members of the Watergate burglary team were among the CIA people involved in the Kennedy assassination.

Later, Haldeman's assistant with his book, *The Ends of Power*, denied that Haldeman made the above statement. Haldeman never denied it.

This was such a fascinating piece of the assassination puzzle that I had to follow-up on it. I decided to contact both Mr. Haldeman and Mr. Helms, even though Mr. Colby's warning was still very fresh on my mind.

Much of what I learned, including the addresses of people I wanted to contact, came straight from the public library. My ability to sift through material at the library was improving. Still, I was unable to locate any information on Mr. Haldeman's whereabouts. I sought the assistance of the library's Information & Referral staff. The librarian commented that it was obvious that Mr. Haldeman did not want to be contacted. Several months later, Mr. Haldeman died. It is very unfortunate that I wasn't able to contact him. A statement by someone who knew he had terminal cancer would have been very credible.

Next, I composed a letter to Mr. Helms. Again, as with Mr. Colby, I referred to Senator John Tower's alleged knowledge of a conspiracy in the Kennedy assassination and the possibility he was murdered. I asked about the involvement of the CIA in the Kennedy assassination.

By this time, I expected a reply from Mr. Helms, based on my success with people such as Colby, Prouty, and Belin. My optimism was rewarded by a call from Mr. Helms a few days after I mailed my letter.

I was at work and returned to my office after a meeting. I checked my voice mail and found that Mr. Helms had left a message for me to call him. I had a copy of the voice mail message made so that I could prove he did, indeed, contact me.

The telephone number I called connected me with the Safeer Corporation, an international consulting firm. It was not unusual for persons retired from the intelligence business to stay in the game and make money using their international connections. I told the receptionist who answered the phone my name, and she said "Mr. Helms is expecting your call."

I said "good morning" to Mr. Helms, and he immediately launched into an authoritarian tirade. Mr. Helms informed me that he read my letter and there was "absolutely no truth in any of it." He reiterated that there was no conspiracy to assassinate the President. So far, this was pretty much what I expected him to say; standard fare for someone who really believed in a lone gunman, or who had something to lose if he had spent his life covering up and profiting from a conspiracy.

Then the phone conversation changed in its character. I wondered if the part about Senator Tower had caught his eye. Mr. Helms' tone of voice took on a threatening tone. He told me, using a very stern tone of voice, that I had "no business investigating this matter." He then told me that Mensa should not allow my involvement. Mr. Helms told me I "had better find something else to do" with my time, and "I had better find a new hobby." It did not take a genius to see this was a thinly veiled threat. Maybe not even thin, and maybe not veiled at all.

At this point, Helms put his hand over the phone and seemed to be talking with someone else in the room. I could not understand what he was saying, but Helms was so angry now that he sounded like he was growling. He continued trying to intimidate me by again telling me to stay out of this matter.

I can understand where Mr. Helms was coming from. I was an average Joe – and he was a powerful man – someone who was used to invoking fear – someone capable of toppling governments and ordering deaths. He no doubt thought I would crumble under his harangue. Mr. Helm's emotional outburst actually had the opposite effect and only made me more curious. (I don't think anyone has intimidated me since I was sixteen years old. Maybe it happened when I grew to be six feet tall. Maybe it's because I'm not smart enough to realize when my life is in danger. In the end, the reason doesn't matter. It's just the way it is.)

After all, if there was no conspiracy to assassinate President Kennedy, and the CIA was completely innocent of any wrongdoing, why could he possibly care if I chose to be yet another person to investigate the conspiracy theory? Why would my free-time activities be of any concern to him? It made no logical sense. Helms, at this point, was so angry that I was afraid he was going to slam the phone down. I thanked him for responding to my letter and asked him if he would consider answering a question. He didn't respond right away so I didn't give him a chance to turn me down.

I asked him about Mr. Haldeman's description of the Watergate-related meeting described in the book *Ends of Power*. I repeated Haldeman's statement about Helms exploding into rage at the mention of "Bay of Pigs."

I was very specific as I further explained that Mr. Haldeman claimed the term "Bay of Pigs" was a code word for the Kennedy assassination, and that members of Watergate burglary team, some of whom had CIA connections, were also involved in the Kennedy assassination.

Mr. Helms's answer was extraordinary.

Helms sounded tired all of a sudden. He seemed to sigh and take a breath. He told me, "Yes, that is correct; that is what happened." Mr. Helms continued speaking, while I sat in stunned silence.

He went on to tell me he remembered the incident at the meeting as clearly as if it were yesterday, and that is "exactly what happened." Based on my description of both the incident and Mr. Haldeman's allegations, it appeared to me that Mr. Helms had just confirmed CIA involvement in the Kennedy assassination.

People make slips from time to time, and I had to give him the chance to take back what he said. I wanted to get the straight story here and was concerned I heard correctly. All he had to say was "You misunderstood" or "That's not what I meant." Helms didn't say either of those.

I reiterated to Mr. Helms what he had just said. He paused. It occurred to me that Mr. Helms did not possess the intellect of a William Colby. Mr. Helms called me with the standard denial etched in his mind, written on paper for all I knew. But when I caught him offguard, he was helpless.

Helms started to wing it, and I don't think it worked very well for him.

"Well," Helms said," the reason I got so excited at Haldeman's statement was that I didn't understand what the term 'Bay of Pigs' meant." I asked Mr. Helms what he thought it was supposed to mean. He said he had no idea. Considering that Mr. Helms was CIA Deputy Director during the Bay of Pigs invasion and was involved in its planning, his explanation was impossible to believe. I asked Mr. Helms why he would get so excited just because someone (Haldeman) said something he didn't understand. Mr. Helms replied that the term "Bay of Pigs" seemed nonsensical to him, and he just didn't understand what it meant. Deciding to go with this train of thought, I said to him, "So the President of the United States told his Chief of Staff to say a nonsensical phrase to you, in the hopes that it would force you do something?" Mr. Helms replied, "That's right. You know if I had ever done anything illegal, I would have gone to jail."

We each said goodbye and another fascinating conversation was over. I have never felt so lied to in a conversation in my life.

The concept that Mr. Helms couldn't think of a meaning for

the "Bay of Pigs" is not plausible. He probably knew more about it than anyone. He didn't even attempt to link it to the ill-fated invasion of Cuba. Mr. Helms, caught offguard for a moment, confirmed Mr. Haldeman's statement about the Bay of Pigs being a code-word for the Kennedy assassination. What that means goes far beyond just a conspiracy in the Kennedy assassination.

The former Director of the CIA confirmed: conspiracy in the Kennedy assassination, CIA involvement, presidential knowledge of the assassination and CIA involvement, a blackmail attempt of the CIA Director by the President of the United States, and failure of these public servants and defenders of the Constitution to bring to justice those responsible for the murder of President Kennedy. When this happens in other countries, don't we call it a coup?

This had turned out to be a very interesting day.

I took very careful notes during our conversation. I had developed my own form of shorthand and wrote as we talked. Afterward, I went over the notes in detail and made sure they matched my recollection to the smallest detail. This was far too important a conversation.

CHAPTER FIVE:
Intelligence Agencies

Now I had a great deal of information. It was time to do something about it. My initial goal was to find the truth. I was certain I was on the right track, and my new goal to seeking justice, or, in this case, indictments.

I had contacted the Mpls. Office of the FBI before Mr. Helms called, with the intent to discuss the information Sam gave me.

I understood the reaction of the FBI when I asked to meet with them to discuss my evidence. I received a not-very polite "no thanks." The Kennedy assassination had, maybe as a result of people's frustration with not knowing the truth, attracted more than its share of "off the wall" types.

Since I worked for a mental health center, I knew what it was like for poor souls, prone to delusions, to relate their stories. I also had been contacted during my research by a fair share of deluded people, including a person who thought he was the deceased David Koresh.

David Koresh, the founder of the Branch Davidians cult, died in a shoot out with Alcohol, Tobacco and Firearms (ATF) agents, who had been alerted to an arsenal of explosives and weapons at the compound in Waco, Texas in 1993.

Determined to make some progress, I contacted my Congressman, Jim Ramstad, and explained the situation to him (1994). Mr. Ramstad contacted the FBI and, I assume with a little arm-twisting, arranged a meeting. I was to contact Mr.

Larry Mefford, Supervisory Special Agent of the Mpls. FBI Office. When I called Mr. Mefford, he made time for an appointment with me. He was very professional and polite about it, although my guess is this is the last thing he wanted to do.

The day of the meeting, I walked over to the FBI office and waited only a few minutes for Mr. Mefford. He came out to greet me, and we walked to a conference room.

Mr. Mefford listened patiently and politely. It was obvious that I was not making much of an impression – until I mentioned the audio tape that Sam claimed Billie Sol Estes had made. Mr. Mefford immediately looked interested. He explained that such a tape would be real evidence, and would be something worth looking into. I concluded my presentation by mentioning the phone calls from Mr. Helms and Mr. Colby, something else that interested Mr. Mefford. He told me "those kinds of people don't call average citizens; they just don't." The combination of the tape plus the phone calls from two CIA Directors succeeded in arousing his curiosity.

Mefford told me that he would give Sam a call and talk with him. He said I could call back in two weeks to find out what progress had been made. Two weeks passed, and I called Mefford. His attitude had changed. He told me that since this matter was a crime which occurred in Dallas, it had been taken out of his hands. He referred me to the Dallas FBI office for further information. I think he was disappointed.

I contacted the Dallas FBI office. They had no information, but promised to get back to me. Six months went by, and I had heard nothing. I wrote a letter to them, and an agent responded with an apology that it had taken so long to get back to me. He promised to get back to me soon. He never did.

As a final follow-up to my dealing with intelligence groups, I contacted Mr. David Whipple, the Executive Director of the

Association of Former Intelligence Officers. The letter I sent him was very brief and to the point.

First, I asked if his organization was of the opinion that intelligence agents could have been involved in the Kennedy assassination. Second, I asked if Oswald had any involvement with intelligence agencies. The Association of Former Intelligence Officers was founded by Mr. David Atlee Phillips. Mr. Phillips, now deceased, was a high level officer of the CIA. He purportedly started the organization because of the bad publicity the CIA was receiving during the 1970's. Mr. Phillips was identified by Mr. Gaeton Fonzi, investigator for the HSCA (House Select Committee on Assassinations), as being with Lee Harvey Oswald in September of 1963.

Mr. Whipple phoned me and immediately told me that "nobody in the association thinks he [Oswald] had any association with intelligence agencies." This seemed like an extraordinarily sweeping statement for someone to make about a large organization. I asked him, "nobody?" Mr. Whipple's reply was "Certainly not. I have checked with a number of people in the association, and they all agree there was no such thing as assassination by the Intelligence Community. There is a Presidential Executive Order forbidding it." I was under the impression that the Executive Order was issued precisely because of evidence that intelligence agencies did indeed attempt to assassinate – Castro, for example.

I then told Mr. Whipple that "your founder" Mr. Phillips was a subject of study for Mr. Gaeton Fonzi, an investigator with the HSCA, and was written about in Fonzi's book *The Last Investigation*. Mr. Whipple said he didn't know Fonzi and had never heard of his book.

Mr. Whipple then continued to discuss the subject of David Atlee Phillips. He said that he knew Mr. Phillips was accused of killing Orlando Letelier. Letelier had been Chile's defense minister when Salvador Allende was overthrown in 1973. He was arrested, tortured, and exiled in 1974, and was the victim of a remote-control bomb attached to his car in 1976. Mr. Phillips was exonerated and was now dead. Why Mr. Whipple brought up this point, I don't know, though it was a central topic of Mr. Fonzi and the matter was described in his book.

I asked Mr. Whipple about Fletcher Prouty's assertion that members of the intelligence community were, indeed, involved in the Kennedy assassination. Mr. Whipple said he had never heard of Prouty and "had no idea who he was." I explained that he handled covert operations for the military, including the Joint Chiefs of Staff during the late 1950's and early 1960's. Mr. Whipple said, "No wonder, I was running stations overseas then."

Mr. Whipple then asked if I was writing in response to publicity concerning John Neumann, who had recently written a book linking Oswald to the CIA. I told him I was not familiar with the book. Mr. Whipple stated that in regards to the subject of the Kennedy assassination "people are only out for publicity." He stated that there are 3,000 members in his association and all are loyal Americans. Mr. Whipple said it was unthinkable that an intelligence officer would break the law or hurt the President. He said their duty was to protect the President.

Mr. Whipple said I was welcome to print our conversation.

Given all that had happened, I decided that someone in authority should look into some of this. I contacted the United States Senate and asked that the allegation be investigated, that a United States Senator had approved the murder of Senator John Tower. For all I knew, the accused senator was one of the most law-abiding men who ever lived. This was a tremendous allegation. I didn't want to embarrass him; however, if true, this was of national importance. I thought the Senate would be able to quietly look into the matter and decide if there was any credence. The reply referred me to law enforcement agencies. Obviously, the Senate didn't want to get involved in such an unpleasant, earth-shattering mess. Who would blame them? The political circus that would result would doubtlessly accomplish nothing.

CHAPTER SIX:
Mike Hall

At this point, my research had pretty much dead-ended. I had contacted most of the people who I thought could reasonably be of help. It seemed that the best thing to do would be to wind down my research group and move on to other subjects.

Then, on March 30, 1995, an editorial in the *Minneapolis Star Tribune* caught my eye. It was a reprint of an article written by an editor of the *Albany Times* newspaper. Its intent, as far as I could determine, was to ridicule anyone who believed there was a conspiracy to murder to President Kennedy. The "whipping boy" in this case was Oliver Stone. The author focused on Stone's upcoming film, *Nixon*, released in 1995.

The article brought to mind my ninth grade Civics class. The instructor, John Jeffries, was intent on helping us to discern whether someone had a good argument or if they were just preying on emotions to get what they wanted.

First, and foremost, my teacher taught, was to consider this: Did the person use evidence, or did he just try to ridicule his opponent? If he just tried to make fun, he probably didn't really believe what he was saying and was just plain desperate. The author of that article struck me as fitting my teachers description to a T. The author rambled on about how Stone was trying to deceive us and take our money, none of which seemed to have anything to do with the subject on hand. I found it outrageous that the *Minneapolis Star Tribune* would reprint such a poorly written article in the paper. I called the *Star Tribune*, and spoke to a representative of the Editorial Board, who listened patiently to my critique of the article. To my surprise, she agreed with me that it was not only misleading, but insulting. She agreed to review a rebuttal letter from me. I immediately composed a letter and sent it in. The letter ran on April 8, 1996. I thought that this would close the issue. It didn't. It reopened the issue wider than I had ever imagined.

For the next two weeks, I received calls at home from a variety of well-wishers. All were polite and well-informed about the assassination. A couple of the people who called had military combat experience and thought it ludicrous that one man could have done that much shooting, and that the President's head and body would have reacted the way they did to a shot coming from the rear.

One person called while I was out and refused to leave a message. I didn't think anything of it, but the person continued to call, always missing me, and each time refusing to leave a message. Finally, one month after my rebuttal letter appeared in the *Star Tribune*, that person did call when I was at home. The information the person related was startling. By now, I had received so many crank calls and letters that it was pretty easy to sort out the delusional people, from those who were well-meaning with nothing new, from those who really had something. This person really had something.

This person had befriended Mr. Mike Hall, a retired Bureau Chief of the Alcohol, Tobacco and Firearms (ATF). Mr. Hall had confided that he was well-connected with the CIA, especially so because of his Miami and New Orleans experience. Miami and New Orleans were staging areas for the CIA's anti-Castro activities.

Mike Hall had told the caller that the CIA had a significant role in the assassination of President Kennedy, and had really done its best work, not just on the killing, but also on the cover-up. According to Mr. Hall, the CIA controlled so many areas of government that a real investigation was next to impossible. Those who dared to conduct a real investigation were "dealt with." The caller then told me that there was no way I was going to find out the caller's identity. (Remember that "caller ID" was not yet generally available to the public.)

The caller assured me that my letter was right-on with the indication that the CIA was a principal in Kennedy's death and warned me to watch out. The caller had been calm, rational, and seemed quite sincere. The problem with figuring out these types of calls is whether this obviously well-meaning person knew what he/she was talking about. If he/she did, if anything he/she said could be confirmed, it would be a tremendous help.

After some thought, I decided to call the St. Paul office of the ATF to check whether there really was such a person as Mike Hall, and whether he was, indeed, a Bureau Chief. Obviously, if no such person existed, I could write off the caller's story as some poor soul's delusion.

I called the ATF office and asked to speak with personnel. The receptionist told me there was no personnel office located there. She asked if I could explain my reason for calling. When I told her I wanted to check on a Mr. Hall, who may have been employed there many years ago, she said, "I'll connect you with Bob Smith (not his real name). He's a senior agent and has been here forever. If anyone would have known Mr. Hall, he would."

Mr. Smith answered his phone, and I quickly introduced myself and asked if he knew of a Mike Hall. Mr. Smith said he knew Mike Hall, and, yes, Mike had been the Bureau Chief at the St. Paul Office. I expected that the last thing this man wanted to hear was the background of my research, so I decided I had enough information. I had confirmed Mr. Hall's existence and his occupation. That gave some credence to the caller's story, and that was all I could have expected to gain from this phone call.

I thanked Mr. Smith for his time and began to say goodbye when he asked me, "Why do you want to know?" I explained that this was going to sound pretty unusual, but someone had told me that Mr. Hall was connected with the CIA and that he knew about CIA involvement in the Kennedy assassination. I expected a chuckle, or maybe a sigh from Mr. Smith.

Instead, he said, "Oh yes, I know all about that." I recovered as best I could. I reiterated what he had just told me. Mr. Smith said that someone, probably the same person who phoned me, had sent him a letter describing Mr. Hall's account of the Kennedy assassination and the CIA involvement therein. I asked Mr. Smith if I could see the material. He said he had it somewhere in his desk, but didn't want to share it. I didn't want to agitate such an unexpectedly helpful source of information, so I did not push him on this. I asked Mr. Smith if he had any idea where Mike Hall was living. He said that Hall was retired from the Bureau and had moved to Florida. He had heard that Hall was trying to start a restaurant and that the restaurant had some financial problems. Mr. Smith didn't know where in Florida Hall was living, but told me that there was a close personal friend I could try to contact. Mr. Smith said, "Find Ed Jones (not his real name); he will know where Hall is. If you find Jones, you'll find Hall. He works for Glynco in Atlanta." Mr. Smith was now sounding strained, possibly regretting having told me so much. He said goodbye and hung up.

For whatever reason, it was not easy finding an address for Glynco. As it turned out, Glynco was an association for retired Federal agents, which was based at or near the ATF training center in Atlanta. (At this point I remember that Senator Tower's plane crashed at Glynco – a fascinating coincidence). I called the ATF training center and asked to speak with Mr. Ed Jones. The receptionist was not familiar with him, but checked an employee listing.

The receptionist told me there was no such person employed there. I insisted that there must be a Ed Jones, so she put me on hold and sought assistance. She came back on the line and told me they were unable to find such a name. Her answer effectively ended my search. This dead end left me with an odd feeling. I knew that somewhere there was another piece to this puzzle.

It took a few days, but I remembered in the book, *The Last Investigation*, by Gaeton Fonzi, that there was some reference to this story. As an investigator for the House Select Committee on Assassinations, his book is one of the few on this subject that deal with actual events, instead of mere speculation. I re-read the book and found, on page 278, a reference to an unnamed Treasury Agent from Minnesota who interfered with Fonzi's investigation. He implied that the Treasury Agent was performing a service for the CIA. I realized that this had to be Hall. I wrote to Mr. Fonzi and asked for information. Fonzi wrote back (July 1995), confirmed that the person he wrote about was Mike Hall, and offered to check with his contacts for information regarding Hall's whereabouts.

The summer passed by quickly, and I was no closer to finding Mr. Hall. I was ready to fly to Florida on a moment's notice to interview him. I felt that if I could talk with him, I'd convince him to let me interview him on tape. I would offer to seal the interview until after his death, if necessary. This would delay the nation knowing the truth, but still, it would be better than nothing. I was making no progress in my search for Hall. I had not heard back from Fonzi, and I had no other leads.

Mr. Fonzi suggested earlier that I contact the Assassination Records Review Board (ARRB) with my information. I was hesitant to do so. First, they had done nothing with the information I had given them about Sam's audio tape. But that isn't what really bothered me.

Most importantly, I didn't want to put Mr. Hall into any danger. Historically, people with information in the Kennedy assassination have wound up, to be blunt, murdered. Sam Giancana, Johnny Roselli and who knows how many others turned up dead when investigated by Congressional Boards. Even one of Mr. Fonzi's potential witnesses (Mr. de Mohrenschildt) died suddenly. Considering that Mr. Hall may have significant information on the Kennedy assassination, which would threaten the status of many powerful people, it seemed best to be cautious. Also troubling, I recalled that a CIA agent was caught breaking into the files of the House Select Committee on Assassinations. It would certainly be as easy to break into the ARRB files.

The idea that Mr. Hall would be a highly credible witness was not lost on me. A retired Bureau Chief testifying that the CIA was involved in the murder of President Kennedy was bound to get the nation's attention, and that would be the best way to finally reveal the truth and get justice.

Finally, I decided that, with my very limited financial resources, the ARRB was the only way Mr. Hall would be found and interviewed. I contacted the ARRB and gave them the information on Mr. Hall. They seemed quite interested and promised to look into it.

Not one to sit around waiting for someone else to do

something, I decided to continue searching for Hall myself. I wrote a letter to Mr. Ed Jones at the ATF Training Center in Glynco, Georgia. My reasoning was that Bob Smith must have known what he was talking about when he referred me there. If Jones was no longer employed there, maybe there was someone in the mailroom who would remember him.

Several days after I mailed the letter, I checked my voice mail and found I had a message from Nita Jones at the ATF Training Center in Glynco, Georgia. I called her. Mrs. Jones told me that her husband, Ed, had asked her to call me. What she said next was crushing.

She reported that Mike Hall had just died unexpectedly. I asked her for details. Mrs. Jones told me that Hall was in perfect health and had no history of health problems. They believed he had a heart attack. He was vacationing with his wife and left one day for a walk in the woods. When he did not return, she went searching for him and found him on the ground.

Mrs. Jones asked me why I was searching for Hall. I explained my reasons, and she was not the least bit surprised. I asked for an address where Mrs. Hall could be reached, and she gave me a P.O. Box. My opportunity for knowledge was quickly slipping away, so I asked Mrs. Jones how her husband knew Mike Hall. She told me that they had worked together for years. Realizing that at least I could get some second-hand information, I told Mrs. Jones I would appreciate the chance to speak with her husband.

Apparently Mrs. Jones was ready for this and immediately told me that her husband did not want to talk with me.

That conversation ended, I contacted Mr. Thomas Samoluk of the ARRB. Mr. Samoluk informed me that a staff person had been assigned to interview Mr. Hall, but had not yet done so. He also informed me that the files at the ARRB were secure and that no one could have reviewed them. Obviously, this was a devastating blow to what could have been a history-writing event.

First, William Colby, and now Mike Hall. I began to believe I was chasing ghosts.

I was determined to follow up as best I could. I contacted ATF Agent Bob Smith again, to discuss the material he had which linked Hall, the CIA and the Kennedy assassination. Mr. Smith was much less helpful this time. I asked him for a chance to review the material. He said, "Uh, I don't think I have it anymore." I asked him where it was. He repeated that he no longer had it and hung up. I was sorry Mr. Smith had changed his mind about helping, but this was a matter that needed to be reviewed.

I filed a Freedom of Information Act (FOIA) with the ATF. A reporter had advised me to send the FOIA to the office where the information was, as this would hasten the search and retrieval of materials. I sent the FOIA to the St. Paul ATF. They forwarded it to Washington, D.C.

Shortly after that, I received a response from the D.C. office that no records existed on the matter I had requested. I immediately appealed, reminding them that an ATF agent in St. Paul had told me that he had the written document I was requesting. It was simple to understand and would have been simple for them to do.

The ATF responded that they did not have the document. I then wrote the ATF and informed them that I understood that the document may no longer exist. I asked them for information as to what happened to the document.

The ATF responded that they did not have to answer my questions. The decision by the ATF not to conduct a legitimate search was both disturbing and frightening. The ATF was refusing to cooperate in the spirit in which the law was intended.

Once again, I contacted Congressman Jim Ramstad and asked for his assistance. Mr. Ramstad intervened, but was quickly put down by the ATF, who insisted they were following the letter, if not the intent, of the law. The ATF was obviously trying to cover up Agent Smith's destruction of the material. This is not only frustrating, it is deeply troubling. The ATF is a government agency whose mission is to serve the American public. Purposely violating Freedom of Information laws and then covering up does not serve the public. It is reasonable to assume that the ATF would not violate laws or cover up those violations if there was no incriminating evidence. If Agent Smith's document did not describe illegal acts, what point would there be in taking the risk the ATF took by violating the law? If the document Agent Smith once had was just a meaningless piece of paper, why would he go to such lengths to prevent me from seeing it? If Mike Hall had no connection to the CIA, no knowledge of CIA conspiracy in the assassination of President Kennedy, then why did Agent Smith tell me he "knew all about that"? Why did Agent Smith encourage me to proceed with my investigation by directing me to Ed Jones? A reasonable person would look at all that went on with the ATF and Mike Hall and be suspicious of illegal activities and cover up.

I contacted a reporter for the local St. Paul paper to discuss the subject of government cover-ups. He referred me to a national watchdog organization located in Washington D.C. I telephoned and spoke with a woman there who handles matters related to government cover-ups. I explained what happened. She was not surprised. She told me that destruction of documents by Federal agents and agencies "happens all the time." She said that persons do this for the obvious reasons – to destroy evidence that could get them into trouble.

Somewhere along the time since I began this investigation, I realized I used to be as naïve as they come. At one time in my life, I would have been stunned by this woman's statement. Now, I realize she was just being straightforward and truthful.

I began a series of Freedom of Information Requests to retrieve the above mentioned document concerning Mike Hall. My quest lasted for years. During this time, I was stonewalled and insulted. Once, when I repeated my conversation with Agent Bob Smith, I received a reply that I had made a "quantum leap" – the implication being that I made up the information, perhaps because I was so excited about talking with a "Federal agent." I'm sorry, but after speaking with Mr. Helms and Mr. Colby, an ATF agent doesn't get my blood pumping any faster. Since Agent Smith told me he knew all about it and had written information about it, I don't think that qualifies as a "quantum leap." It was no comfort to realize tax dollars go to an organization that insults citizens.

Since the ATF trail was hopeless, I contacted the CIA. I asked for information linking Mike Hall with the CIA. My request was denied. I appealed, stating that Mr. Hall had died unexpectedly, shortly after I gave his name to the ARRB for an investigative interview. Wow – that got their attention, and they accepted my appeal.

Finally, after years of filing Freedom of Information Requests and appeals, I received a letter from the CIA that ended this part of the search. Their reply was, "the fact of the existence or nonexistence of any documents (concerning the relationship of Mike Hall to the CIA) which would be responsive to that portion of your request for records that would divulge a confidential or covert relationship...is classified.... By this statement we are neither confirming or denying that any such documents exist."

So whether or not Mike Hall did indeed perform some services for the CIA remains

unknown. My impression is that Gaeton Fonzi believes Hall did help the CIA interfere in his

investigation for the House Select Committee on Assassinations. The person who called and informed me about Mike Hall stated the same thing. Coincidence? It doesn't seem likely. Given Mike Hall's history of working in Florida and New Orleans, it is quite likely he may have made contact with the CIA. If he did have CIA contacts, even occasionally worked for the CIA, he likely spoke the truth when he claimed knowledge of CIA complicity in the Kennedy assassination.

CHAPTER SEVEN:
Loose Ends

A member of my Mensa SIG wrote me an interesting letter. He tells a tragic story about a friend of his who worked for Lyndon Johnson. The friend, Wallace Engle, allegedly committed suicide after LBJ became President. Apparently, there was some dispute whether the death was self-inflicted. The article the SIG member enclosed with the letter was from *The Sacramento Bee*, Friday, December 1966, page D4, titled "Former LBJ Aide Is Apparent Suicide." I contacted the next of kin, who was still alive at the time, but received no answer back. There are so many mysterious deaths associated with the JFK assassination that a reasonable person would question, "Are they all accidents or suicides?" What is really unfortunate is that so much was left unexplored in so many deaths. Are there even more mysterious deaths that have not become public knowledge? How many more Wallace Engle's have there been?

The letter is both sad and stunning. It raises questions about President Lyndon Johnson. I have tried to research this event but haven't had much luck.

When I first started my investigation, one of the first people I wrote to was Congressman Henry Gozalez (Texas). He served as Chair of the House Select Committee on Assassinations. Mr. Gonzalez did not last long on the committee as political infighting raged supreme. Mr. Gonzalez wrote to me and expressed disappointment that "dark forces" had sabotaged the work of the committee. He encouraged me to carry on with my research.

Another line of inquiry I pursued had some commonality with research done by another, relatively famous JFK investigator. I wrote a friendly letter to the researcher, explaining that I had the same interest he did and perhaps he could offer some guidance or share some information. I never expected the reply I received. It seems he was greatly offended that I was treading on his turf. Assistance? Not going to come from him. Still, it was an interesting and eye-opening experience.

In another attempt, I contacted Senator Barry Goldwater about a statement he once made that Lyndon Johnson had made a lot of money during his presidency – Goldwater said he didn't know how, but Johnson did make a lot of money. Goldwater is one of the few people that never returned my inquiry. That is too bad. I wondered if Goldwater was implying that something outside the law had happened.

I am convinced that there was significant photographic evidence of the assassination that the public never saw. Evidence of a much better quality than the Zapruder film probably was taken by the crowd at Dealey Plaza.

In 1996, when my father died, I found in his belongings a 1963 newspaper article about a man who lived near my small hometown of Hoyt Lakes, Minnesota. The man had since died, but I spoke with his son. According to the son, his father took a movie picture that included Dealey Plaza from the opposite angle of the Zapruder film. This would show the sequence of shots better than the Zapruder film and may have shown a unique angle of the grassy knoll. This man heard two distinct shots from the direction of the grassy knoll. The film was taken from him that day by someone who identified himself as a government agent. After his film was confiscated, the man crossed the street to the steps of the Texas Book Depository and bumped into someone who was calm but determined in his mannerism. He later identified that man as Lee Harvey Oswald. The man made a death bed statement, in a videotape recorded for his son, that everything he said was true.

One wonders if somewhere there is evidence that has not yet been uncovered. A photograph, still picture, some evidence that someone stashed away either because they were afraid for their personal safety or just didn't know what to do. There may be persons still alive who have personal knowledge of events – and are afraid to come forward. Perhaps something or someone will come to light in the next few years.

Another subject of speculation regarding the Kennedy assassination cover-up has been the role of CBS. Researchers have found that at one time, upper management at CBS and CIA have socialized together. If true, this could be innocent, yet gives rise to the suspicion that news reporting may be biased, a contention of Bernard Goldberg in his 2002 book, *Bias: A CBS Insider Exposes How the Media Distort the News.*

Obviously, if the CIA was involved in the Kennedy assassination, a cozy relationship between this covert agency and the CBS network would greatly enhance the cover-up. One can imagine the CIA telling CBS executives that a cover-up is necessary for the "good of the country."

Reporters are trained observers, and as a reporter, Dan Rather (now CBS news anchor) was eyewitness to the assassination. Mr. Rather has publicly stated that, although he was at the scene at the time of (or immediately after) the assassination, he did not notice anything. Mr. Rather apparently did not realize that a shooting and a murder was occurring. It would be fair to give Mr. Rather the benefit of the doubt about this. Some people do not deal well with the unexpected, and maybe Mr. Rather is one of those people. Perhaps when Mr. Rather has time to prepare for an interview, write the news in advance of reading it, etc., he does quite well, while unexpected events throw him off.

Unfortunately, the above explanation does not answer the question as to what happened when Mr. Rather reported on the Zapruder film to the American people.

Mr. Rather was one of the few people allowed to see the Zapruder film. He reported to the American people that when the "killing shot" hit Mr. Kennedy, his head snapped forward. This statement strongly confirmed the Warren Commission conclusions and seemed intended to reassure the American public that all was well. The problem with that statement, of course, is that it was undeniably 100% wrong. Mr. Kennedy's head snaps backwards when he is hit by the final shot, not forward. Even supporters of the Warren Commission do not dispute this fact.

At first blush, Mr. Rather appears to have mis-reported what he saw on the Zapruder film. Again, not knowing his true intentions, it may lead to the suspicion that he was trying to cover-up the fact of conspiracy.

The supporters of the Warren Commission were able to find a doctor who testified before Congress that the President's backward snap was the result of neurological damage, caused by the bullet. It is quite true that such damage can cause any number of awkward bodily movements; however, this does not explain the immediate thrust of the President's head. Simply put, the head moves in whatever direction it is pushed. Had the head been pushed from behind, as the Warren Commission contends, it would have snapped forward and then, only then, would the neurological damage have forced the head to snap in a different direction. When an "expert" comes up with a claim that is totally against all common sense, it may be best not to believe the "expert."

The situation, then, is that Mr. Rather saw the Zapruder film, saw the President's head violently snap backwards, yet reported that it snapped forwards. What he reported did not happen. Millions of Americans were given his statement as fact, when the fact was completely opposite.

When confronted about this years later, when the Zapruder film was available to the public, Mr. Rather said he made a mistake. This was not an instance where Mr. Rather was taken by surprise; it was not an unexpected event. He knew that he was going to see a film of the death of the President. He knew that the American public would be depending on him for the truth. He had ample time to prepare and accurately report on what happened. Mr. Rather gave a report which was false. Again, this appears to be a willful cover-up of the truth, the motive being to keep the American people in the dark. Mr. Rather's major mistake, something that could end a career, has not held him back. He has become a wealthy, famous anchorman for CBS. Years later, when the movie *JFK* came out, Mr. Rather devoted an episode of a prime time news show to proving that the Warren Commission was correct.

The end of the show consisted of him sitting with one of his reporters (read – employees) discussing the "fact" that Oswald was the lone assassin and the Warren Commission was correct. The reporter nodded his head so vigorously as Mr. Rather spoke that it appeared to me to be a staged event.

Walter Cronkite, a respected newsman at CBS for many years, interviewed retired President Johnson in 1969. During the interview, Mr. Johnson implied strongly that the Warren Commission did not tell the full truth and that there was a conspiracy involved in President Kennedy's death. Rumors have since spread about this interview, claiming that far more was said during the interview than was broadcast. I decided to look into this. The "news show" conducted by Dan Rather had part of the interview between Johnson and Cronkite. Mr. Rather chose not to pursue this lead, however – something which one would assume a good investigative reporter would fiercely jump on.

First, I wrote the Lyndon Johnson library and asked for a copy of the transcript. I received the transcript, but the part of the interview which I saw on TV was completely omitted. I wrote the library, pointing out that the transcript they sent was incomplete (see appendix, document 11). They indicated that what they sent was all they had. Another amazing coincidence?

I then wrote CBS and asked for a transcript. I was sent transcripts from other interviews conducted in 1970. None had anything to do with the interview I saw on TV. I contacted CBS and explained that they had sent the wrong transcript. I again specifically explained what I was looking for. They then sent me a transcript of Mr. Cronkite interviewing President Johnson about the Space Program.

I then contacted Mr. Rather, thinking perhaps they would have access to a transcript of the program. He has never replied to my request.

I wrote Mr. Cronkite's assistant, asking Mr. Cronkite to take the opportunity to comment on the part of the interview where Mr. Johnson talked about the inaccuracies of the Warren Commission and a conspiracy. His assistant replied that Mr. Cronkite addressed President Johnson's statement by saying he did not understand what [President Johnson] was trying to say.

CHAPTER EIGHT:
Judge John Tunheim's Talk

So what is a citizen who is interested in the Kennedy assassination to do? Maybe you are a fervent believer in the Warren Commission Report. Perhaps you are certain that President Kennedy was murdered by a conspiracy. Or maybe you are undecided.

One road you may choose would be to research the matter and learn as much as you can. It's easier than you might think to investigate. Thanks to movie director Oliver Stone, the Assassination Records Review Board (ARRB) was created by an act of Congress (1992). This happened because Stone's 1991 movie, *JFK*, caused a great debate about what really happened in Dallas on November 22, 1963.

Once the act was passed by Congress, it was up to then-President Clinton to choose a person to lead the review board. He chose John Tunheim. Federal Judge Tunheim interviewed with Clinton and told him he didn't have more than an average citizen's knowledge of the events of the assassination. Clinton told him that was what he was looking for. Judge Tunheim went into this job with no axe to grind.

The ARRB amassed an impressive archive of material during the few years they were in existence. All of this material is available through the National Archives. The location of the material is at the University of Maryland in College Park, Maryland. But one does not have to travel to gain access. Much of the information is accessible via the World Wide Web (http://www.archives.gov/research_room/jfk/index.html). So, if you are interested, and have some time, access the site and learn about the assassination.

There is a small, but well-run group in the Minneapolis-St. Paul area that meets several times a year to learn and share information about the Kennedy assassination. On February 24, 2003 Judge Tunheim spoke to this group. I was in attendance. At no time did the judge say either "There was a conspiracy" or "There was not a conspiracy."

Judge Tunheim apparently has long ago decided to let the evidence speak for itself.

I've summarized below much of what he had to say that evening. The remainder of this chapter is simply the text from my notes of Judge John Tunheim's presentation, and is not meant to be in a formal fashion.

"The sole purpose of the Warren Commission was to preempt other investigations. They (the Warren Commission) knew nothing about Operation Mongoose, or Cuban issues, and took no serious look at organized crime. They were politicians, not investigators." (Operation Mongoose was a code name for a CIA plot to kill Fidel Castro. Richard Helms was involved. The plot failed. It is thought by some that Castro may have sought revenge for the attempts on his life.)

J. Lee Rankin's files showed several drafts of the Warren Commission report. Tunheim believes this indicates they were trying to script evidence in a believable fashion around a preconceived conclusion. (J. Lee Rankin was general counsel for the Warren Commission.)

The judge obviously had little respect for the Warren Commission as anything but a political body. He felt that it was a great mistake to place them in a position of resolving a crime of national importance.

On the subject of the House Select Committee that studied President Kennedy's assassination in the 1970's, Tunheim commented, "They quit too soon." This committee came up with exactly the opposite conclusion of the Warren Commission. Much of the conclusion was based on the recording of gunshots at Dealey Plaza. At least four gunshots were recorded on the tape. There are additional sounds on the tape that may be more shots, but there is no agreement on this. (The Warren Commission found only three spent gun shells in the Texas Book Depository. This begs the question, where did the fourth shot come from?)

"The House Select Committee also investigated the murder of Dr. Martin Luther King. This Committee was besought by 'outside forces' from its beginning. Someone did not want the Committee to investigate."

"The CIA ran a massive investigation on the assassination immediately afterwards, and shared virtually nothing with the Warren Commission."

He seemed genuinely shocked that such a thing could happen. He gave an example of the thoroughness of the CIA investigation by stating that even agents in Jerusalem who heard something on the street would write it down on a slip of paper and forward it to headquarters.

George de Mohrenschildt, who appeared to have some link to the CIA and to Lee Harvey Oswald, died after being contacted by a Congressional investigator (Gaeton Fonzi). The death was ruled a suicide. (I had asked Mr. Colby about Mr. de Mohrenschildt.)

A CIA agent was captured breaking into the files of the House Select Committee. Very little was made of what should have been a major scandal.

James Angleton was the CIA Chief of Counterintelligence. Angleton was "a spooky guy, one of the worst lawbreakers," in Tunheim's opinion. Unfortunately, Angleton took over the CIA investigation of the Kennedy assassination. Angleton's files were burned when he died, and he probably burned some before he died.

Tunheim related a story that Ben Bradley, former editor of the *Washington Post*, told about finding Angleton at the apartment of a girl who was murdered (a supposed friend of JFK). Angleton was sorting through her stuff and took her diary. Bradley was stunned to find Angleton there, and equally stunned that he would take something and leave.

It appeared to Tunheim that the CIA thought it could out-wait the ARRB. Since the ARRB had a limited existence, by law, all the CIA had to do was wait. And they did. The CIA waited until the last day of the ARRB existence to hand over a memo by James Schlesinger, former CIA Director. The memo said he would not allow himself to get into trouble by giving false testimony and wanted information about the "family jewels" – alleged chronicles of CIA wrongdoing. (The implication here is that Schlesinger knew about secret files, but even as a former director, could not access them.)

The FBI and CIA taped what was supposedly Oswald conversing with the Cuban and Russian embassies in Mexico City. This could prove/disprove a lot, but the tapes have vanished. (One pivotal point of the Warren Commission Report is that Oswald went to Mexico City. Yet, no evidence was ever presented to confirm this. At one point, the CIA claimed to have a photo of Oswald in Mexico City, but it was obviously not him.)

The FBI tried to intimidate critics of the Warren Commission, for example Mark Lane. (Mark Lane is a longtime critic of the

Warren Commission. He has written books and articles pointing out the flows in the Warren Report.)

It's fairly well-known that J. Edgar Hoover, the FBI Director from 1924 to 1972, when he died, kept files on people. He remains a mysterious and sometimes vilified man. Some Hoover files were found, but the most secret of his files were destroyed by his secretary and his partner.

The Secret Service destroyed many documents when the ARRB asked for them. The Secret Service claimed they were just doing routine housecleaning.

The KGB still has extensive files. They were worried they were going to be framed for the assassination. Yeltsin released 120 pages, but then "something" changed. Perhaps Russia worried we would see a pattern as to how they conducted spying. (I have contacted the Russian embassy a number of times and have attempted other contacts with Russians to try to gain access to some of the information. So far, not much luck.)

Regarding mobster Sam Giancana: "We paid him big money to kill Castro and spent big money to convict him. He felt betrayed." Giancana was killed in Chicago the night before he was to appear at the Senator Church committee interview. (Senator Church was investigating CIA misdeeds in 1973).

Also on organized crime, Tunheim brought up the name Sam Trafficante and said they had "very interesting stuff" about this man. A former mob lawyer claimed several years ago that he carried a message between Trafficante and Giancana. The message said that Kennedy would be murdered in the fall of 1963.

Judge Tunheim commented on the often maligned New Orleans investigation by Jim Garrison. "Garrison had some good stuff but was an inept investigator, he didn't know what to do with what he had." (If one watches the movie *JFK*, one will see a confirmation by Jim Garrison, himself, of that opinion. Garrison made no secret of his shortcomings.) Garrison himself stated that the investigation is "beyond him." He makes a comparison to his staff being like "children" in a complex situation.

There was quite a hassle getting Garrison's records. People in New Orleans were surprised that some of Garrison's records still existed. Someone forwarded the records to Tunheim, much to the displeasure of the current New Orleans District Attorney. Tunheim got into legal trouble with the New Orleans District Attorney and joked that fortunately he did not plan on traveling to New Orleans at any time in the near future.

Members of Clay Shaw's family donated his diary to the ARRB, and it's a fascinating read. Clay Shaw was slowly coming to the realization he would go to trial for the murder of President Kennedy. (Jim Garrison, the New Orleans District Attorney, arrested and indicted Clay Shaw for the murder of President Kennedy in 1967. Clay Shaw is the only person who was tried for the murder of JFK. He was tried in 1969 and acquitted. Richard Helms revealed under oath in the 1970's that Clay Shaw did indeed perform work for the CIA.)

A Mr. Manchester interviewed "everyone." Manchester is still alive, but elderly and sick. He won't release his records.

Caroline Kennedy was ready to release her version of the records, but someone, probably her uncle Ted Kennedy, talked her out of it.

About the Zapruder film: There were some discrepancies in the film, but it seems like "they" have pretty much put it back together. Kodak reviewed the film, and it seems close to the original. "The Justice Department ineptness cost the taxpayers $16 million."

Lots of film of events surrounding the assassination was

thrown out by local TV studios in Dallas. This was standard editing procedure, but may have resulted in the loss of much valuable information. Some of the film was taken home by employees, and the ARRB was able to retrieve much of this film.

On the grassy knoll, there was no physical evidence, i.e. shell casings left there. However, many people pointed to that area and thought a shot came from there.

The Dallas Police caught Oswald through luck. Ruby spent the weekend at the police station. When Oswald said, "I've been framed," the camera panned and showed Ruby standing nearby. Tunheim contends the Dallas Police were "strictly Mayberry RFD." They were corrupt, poorly trained, and didn't do much investigating.

The autopsy medical records are "very suspicious, there are inconsistencies throughout, 80-90 pictures taken, only 12 exist." The pictures that exist indicate a back entrance wound in the head. (There was no discussion about the claims of falsified pictures, but that may be what he meant by "very suspicious.") A *Washington Post* article about the autopsy pictures is reprinted in the *Minneapolis Star Tribune*, Tuesday, November 10, 1998, on page A13, Report shows discrepancies in brain exams in JFK's autopsy.

All of the attending doctors at Parklawn Hospital on November 22, 1963 are still alive. "All but one emphatically say the throat wound was an entrance wound."

Regarding the Carcano rifle, Tunheim said, "It is possible to shoot three times in five seconds, but not with accuracy." Marine Corps records show Oswald was, at best, a fair shot. Tunheim commented the Carcano rifle was "not much good; if you want something good from Italy get wine, not rifles."

The most haunting question for Tunheim was, "Why did

two identical bullets react so differently? According to the Warren Commission, "One [bullet] hit Kennedy's head and smashed into a hundred pieces. One hit several large bones and is pristine." He examined the bullet and found it absolutely pristine. The magic bullet theory makes no sense whatsoever to Judge Tunheim.

The magic bullet theory is the much-ridiculed idea that one bullet could have caused so much damage to two people and yet remain in pristine condition. The bullet allegedly went into Kennedy (site disputed), came out at an upward angle, entered Governor Connally at a downward angle, smashed his ribs and wristbone, and lodged in his thigh. The bullet, which they claimed did all this damage, was itself unmarked. Tests by the Warren Commission could not duplicate this, as bullets fired into human bones are severely damaged.

Tunheim said, "Either the single bullet theory is correct, or there was a conspiracy. There wasn't time to shoot twice in that amount of time – the Zapruder film proves it." The single bullet theory is another name for the magic bullet theory.

Perhaps the most important thing that Judge Tunheim had to say was, "It is possible there are still some real gems in the 5 million pages of documents" stored in the National Archives, and they are available to everyone.

I found Judge Tunheim's talk to be nothing short of fascinating. He focused on the major finds of the ARRB and some important pieces of evidence. But he also was quite clear that there was a tremendous amount of material that no one has had time to study. And there may be some important information that no one has yet pieced together.

CHAPTER NINE:
Deep Throat

I continued to marvel at how the government of the United States, with virtually unlimited resources, missed the things that I, an average citizen with very limited resources, had learned about the Kennedy assassination. One thing that interested me about the alleged link between the Watergate burglars and the Kennedy assassination was the missing eighteen and a half minutes of tape from Nixon's "secret taping system."

I sent President Nixon a letter describing my research and conversations and asked him to consider the benefit to this country if he had information that could be used to clear up the thirty-year controversy. One week after I mailed my letter, President Nixon died of a stroke. That ended that.

During my investigation, I had come into contact with a journalist who had quite a bit of experience covering the national scene in Washington. I sent him a letter explaining my ongoing investigation and the research I had conducted. I got right to the point – I thought that Deep Throat, whoever he or she was, may have some knowledge about the alleged link between JFK and the Watergate burglars. I acknowledged that the likelihood of one person with no resources finding and interviewing Deep Throat was incredibly small – but no smaller than the likelihood of my getting Richard Helms to admit CIA complicity in the assassination of President Kennedy.

After the Watergate break-in, an unknown person gave information to two *Washington Post* reporters (Bob Woodward and Carl Bernstein). This information was key to the investigation that eventually led to President Nixon's resignation. The identity of the informant was never revealed by Woodward or Bernstein – they referred to the informant only as Deep Throat. It is generally theorized that Deep Throat was a member of the White House staff.

The journalist was helpful. He was someone who genuinely enjoyed helping people and mentoring others to be successful. As it turned out, he was far more helpful that I expected.

It seems he, and some of the people he knew, had a pretty good idea who Deep Throat was. The journalist pushed me in the right direction, and I pursued the lead.

I will refer to Deep Throat by using the masculine "he/him/ etc. This does not mean Deep Throat is a male, not a female. It just makes it easier to write about while still maintaining the person's anonymity.

I followed my usual method of operation. I researched the person that was considered most likely to be Deep Throat. He was, of course, a member of the White House staff. There was no question that he would have considerable access to events in the White House. It seemed like a good probability.

I wrote a brief letter to the person I suspected of being Deep Throat, telling him about my investigation and what I hoped to accomplish by talking with him. I was clear that I wasn't interested in Watergate, per se, but in the Kennedy assassination. I told him I had no "Watergate axe to grind" and that I wasn't interested in hassling him about that incident. As always, I was prepared to either hear nothing from him or receive a form letter telling me to quit bothering him.

About one week later, I received a letter from Deep Throat. There was a short, typewritten message in the envelope. The message said, "call me," and gave me a phone number.

I called Deep Throat. He answered, and I identified myself. But I had a surprise coming. Before I could launch into my questions, he gave me the ground rules. First, we would discuss how I had to come to the conclusion that he was Deep Throat. Second, I would not connect his name with the term "Deep Throat." His identity was, and would remain, a secret.

It had not occurred to me that he would be insistent on this, but of course the reason is obvious. Someone who has worked so hard to remain anonymous would be desperate to know how his identity was revealed.

I explained the legwork I had done. I verified Deep Throat's involvement in, and access to, the Nixon White House. The historical significance of Nixon's presidency being what it was, there was no shortage of biographical information available on everyone who had anything to do with it.

Deep Throat seemed satisfied with my story, and maybe even a little impressed that I had accomplished as much as I did.

I asked if I could begin asking my questions. I asked him about the eighteen and a half minutes. His knowledge of the material was such that obviously he had listened to the tape. This led to another question. I had read that the standard procedure in the White House was to make a copy of the tapes. I asked him if he had a copy of the tape. Deep Throat didn't want to answer that question. Since he was doing me a favor, I didn't feel I could be too demanding, so I gave up that line of questioning.

I asked if President Kennedy's name, or the assassination, was specifically mentioned on the tape. Deep Throat said neither were specifically mentioned. I asked about the "Bay of Pigs" remark. He said that much of what was discussed on the tape was about how to cover-up, not so much specifics about what was covered up. Deep Throat said that there were a lot of generalities that, taken out of context, could either mean nothing or be considered criminal. Given the attitude of the nation at that point in time, it was obvious that the country would choose the latter definition.

I asked Deep Throat if there was anything at all that was discussed on the tape that had to do with the Kennedy assassination. He felt that it was possible that some aspects of the Kennedy assassination cover-up were a part of what Nixon was speaking about.

Departing for a minute from the tape, I asked him about H.R. Haldeman's contention that the term "Bay of Pigs" was a code word for the Kennedy assassination. Deep Throat was familiar with this and believed it possible that there were, indeed, ties between Watergate and the Kennedy assassination. Again, it was likely that Haldeman knew what he was talking about. However, Deep Throat did not know where Haldeman got this information from.

We continued discussing the eighteen and a half minutes of tape. Deep Throat continued to show a thorough knowledge of exactly what was on the tape. His conclusion was this:

First, the conversation on the tape would be interpreted by virtually everyone as containing criminal statements by President Nixon on the need to obstruct justice. Second, there were statements, purposely open-ended and vague. This could be construed as providing a link between Watergate and the Kennedy assassination, but he wasn't going to take the step of saying so.

Sometimes what someone refuses to say is as important as what they do say. The statements made by Deep Throat provided some measure of confirmation to me of Richard Helms's comments about members of the Watergate burglary team being involved in the Kennedy assassination. It was at this point I accomplished everything I had hoped to achieve. Deep Throat had gone out on a limb for me, and I didn't want to take up any additional time. I thanked him for helping me. The next thing I expected was that he would say "goodbye" and hang up. He didn't do so; it seemed like he had something else he wanted to say. I stayed on the line, hoping I could handle an awkward moment without offending him.

I think that after all these years, Deep Throat wanted, needed, someone to talk with about the events that affected him and the country.

Deep Throat told me that he had some regrets over what happened. He did what he thought was best for his country, but it was an emotionally difficult time for him. He had strong feelings that his disloyalty to President Nixon was akin to being a traitor. The turmoil in the country was nothing compared to the emotional turmoil he went through. Deep Throat concluded by saying he wished he could forget about what he did. Years had gone by, and it still caused him a great deal of grief. To this day he continues to try to put it past him, sometimes with very little success.

Deep Throat was and still is considered by many people to be a national hero. The sadness and regret he voiced really gave me pause.

CHAPTER TEN:
Phone Tap?

Finally, I think it's worth mentioning what must be a common occurrence to anyone who has spent time researching the Kennedy assassination. I am referring here to the offbeat conspiracy theorists. Some of these people are naïve and are honestly trying to be helpful. Some have over-active imaginations and get carried away. Unfortunately, some of these people also have mental disorders. I write this chapter not to ridicule these folks but to share the full experience of a Kennedy assassination researcher. A person investigates JFK's death, one really opens his life to some bizarre and unexpected happenings, and becomes a magnet for all sorts of people. A JFK investigator becomes the magnet for all sorts of people. Whether they have an axe to grind or are delusional, they think that an investigator of this subject is someone they must talk to.

Normally, I tend to be a very skeptical person. My typical response when someone tells me they see ghosts, have been abducted by little green men, rent their basement to Elvis, know some information about the Kennedy assassination, is to doubt them. This is not to say I don't believe that such things are possible. I just need proof. Take me into your basement, show me Elvis, let me listen to him sing "Hound Dog," and I'll become a believer. Likewise, show me a ghost, let me ride on the UFO, and I'm on your team.

That's why everyone who approached me with information

about JFK's death was not greeted with eagerness, but with a healthy dose of skepticism. It took quite a bit for me to become a believer that a conspiracy was involved in Kennedy's death.

Here are some of the interactions that failed my reality test and fueled my skepticism.

My investigation was only a few weeks old when I received a letter from a gentleman out East. It seems he knew the real truth about the death of JFK. Because of this information, he claimed that several men, dressed in black and ostensibly working for the government, broke into his house. The men proceeded to insert quite a few electrodes into his brain. With these electrodes they were able to read his thoughts and control his actions. The poor soul never did explain how he was able to write a letter if indeed these mystery men were controlling his thoughts and actions. I'm afraid all I've been able to do for this man, and others like him, is to pray for them.

Another person wrote me to say that he saw the "real" version of the Zapruder film. In this version a Texas cowboy jumped out into the street and pulled two six-shooters and began firing. The cowboy, according to this person, actually was a very poor shot and accidentally killed several bystanders. (Hmmm, a poor shot. Maybe the cowboy was Oswald!) Anyway, the person, of course, did not bother to explain the minor details of how he came upon this film, why he didn't share the film, and why no one noticed or cared about the several bodies of civilians that were strewn around Dealey Plaza.

Several months into my investigation, I began receiving regular phone calls from a gentleman who had done significant research on some minute detail of the assassination. I spent quite a bit of time listening to his claims. Eventually, as one might expect, he told me that he needed to see me privately. There was no way I was going to meet alone with this person, considering I had no idea what his intentions were. Finally, in the hope that he would be satisfied and allow us to go our separate ways, I agreed to meet with him in a public place. I chose a mall on a Sunday afternoon. The gentleman appeared as agreed. He carried a stack of documents so huge that it took both arms to carry. He could barely see over the top of the papers. He placed the papers down on the bench we sat on, and my first thought was, "it will take days to sift through all these documents."

The gentleman began with the top page and did, indeed, intend to discuss each and every piece of paper. I gave him an hour of attention and still had no idea what he was talking about. He had done a great deal of research about something, although I was never able to figure out what. I am certain that it had little, if anything, to do with the Kennedy assassination.

Someone who was very mad at Kennedy for his alleged affair with Marilyn Monroe was certain that there was some sort of Hollywood connection, or perhaps a connection involving Joe DiMaggio. It was an interesting angle and showed great creativity. Somehow, I just couldn't imagine the folks in Hollywood putting together anything other than an awards ceremony. And Joltin' Joe, well, he did have athletic skills. Maybe he could run down all those flights of stairs in time to buy a bottle of soda like Oswald supposedly did. But I don't think he could control the Warren Commission.

Perhaps the most interesting contact I had was in 1994 from someone claiming to be David Koresh. This was the gentlemen who ran a cult near Waco, Texas. He and many of his followers were killed in a clash with the government in 1993. When the person claiming to be David Koresh wrote to me in 1994, he never explained how he survived the fire or how he could be writing letters when he was dead.

His stationery got my attention. It was imprinted "Witness Protection Program" on the top of the page. Now this is a puzzler. Is Mr. "Koresh" so dense he thinks anyone would be fooled by this? The government is a bit inefficient at times, but it's a stretch to think they put "Witness Protection" on their stationary. What's next, "Witness Protection Program" T-shirts? That kind of defeats the purpose.

I shared one of Mr. "Koresh's" letters with a psychologist I worked with. He read the letter over and said the writer appeared to have a thought disorder.

And rage is very much in fashion. When someone would contact me and relate a story that I couldn't agree with, suddenly I became one of "them." The fact that I questioned their story about Kennedy being the sole remaining survivor of the alien crash at Roswell. The fact that I didn't believe the government killed Kennedy to keep him from telling the world he was from the Orion system. My reluctance to believe these "facts" told the caller that I was really on the side of the bad guys. And maybe, just maybe, I was pretending to be an investigator when really I'm only trying to find out who *knows* the truth.

An interesting example of how the bizarre and odd sometimes seem to develop into reality happened to me. I received an interesting letter postmarked from a city in Japan that houses a military base. The writer claimed to be with the military and cautioned me to be careful, especially because my phone was tapped. This isn't the first time someone had told me that – but it was the first time I had someone stationed at a military base in Japan tell me that. I didn't know what to make of it, but oddly enough, a few days after that I began to have terrible trouble with my phone. The line kept cutting in and out. I called the phone company, and they promised to send a repairman. A man in an unmarked, plain white van pulled up in my driveway, climbed the telephone pole, and, poof, no more phone problems. Okay, that did seem odd. I have seen so many phone company trucks and vans around town that it seemed unusual they would have one without any sign. But maybe they just didn't have time to paint it. So whether the letter from Japan had any credence, I can't say.

Still, regardless of the claims, I always tried to be patient and compassionate with anyone who felt strongly about the subject and took the time to contact me. After all, they're as entitled to their beliefs as anyone else. I would hope that anyone who contacted me felt I respected their opinion, regardless of whether or not I agreed with it. Again, for those folks who may have been experiencing some sort of disorder, I can offer only my prayers.

Regardless of the time spent with these folks, I never felt my time was wasted. And I am glad everyone who contacted me did so.

As in the case with this kind of investigation, I still have a story or two that people may find interesting – but I can't print them – at least not now. Nothing that would conclusively prove anything, yet interesting stories about government hijinks and amazing coincidences. The people involved have asked me not to say anything at this time, and I won't.

CHAPTER ELEVEN:
Final Thoughts

Regarding the assassination of President Kennedy – I have no concrete proof in hand that he was killed as the result of a conspiracy. No one, to my knowledge, does have such proof.

Not because such proof never existed – it might have. There is no proof because much of it was destroyed. Several films of the assassination were destroyed by the government. They said it was accidental. The President's brain was removed from its "sealed" storage. There is no explanation from the government on how that happened. Several persons with possible knowledge of conspiracy were either murdered, committed suicide, or died accidentally. The House Select Committee on Assassinations was hampered from the very beginning by persons who obviously didn't want the truth to be told. Government agencies destroyed information and stonewalled investigators.

At some point, everyone has the right to say "enough is enough." How much evidence has to disappear, how many incredible coincidences have to happen, how many people have to die before one says that such an ongoing pattern cannot reasonably or logically be termed a coincidence? Isn't that existing ongoing pattern itself evidence enough to suggest that a conspiracy existed – and continues?

Sometimes, and this is one of those times – a person can and should make a reasonable judgement about the truth. The American public has a great capacity to see the truth. The polls taken on the subject of President Kennedy's death show the public overwhelmingly believes the truth is a conspiracy took place. I have seen nothing to persuade me that they are wrong – quite the opposite.

I would like to give a heartfelt "Thank you" to the many people who willingly shared their time and information. Dr. Cyril Wecht kindly took time from his busy day to phone me and discuss the Mike Hall situation. Mr. Gaeton Fonzi was very helpful to me. Sam Giancana, nephew of the late mobster Sam Giancana, kindly took the time to reply to a letter I wrote. Col. Fletcher Prouty was very helpful over the years. Robert McNamara penned a very short reply that he supported the Warren Commission Report – I appreciated getting his viewpoint. I also approached the nephew of Allen Dulles – and while he had little to share, it was kind of him to take the time to reply (see appendix, document 12). A special thanks to all the members of Mensa who supported the investigation. And, of course, I give my support and encouragement to everyone who desires information and truth. The list of those to acknowledge is lengthy; if your name isn't here, please know that you have earned my gratitude.

THE END

EPILOGUE

When you write something for other people to read, you put part of yourself in that document. Likewise, when you write a book that is controversial, as this book surely is, you put yourself on the firing line.

Doubtless there are people who will not be pleased by this book. I wrote this book because I thought sharing the knowledge I've gained would be helpful and interesting to the American people, who surely – after forty years – deserve to know whatever of the truth is able to be discovered. There are those who prefer to live in a state of denial, and I accept that. Maybe a "head in the sand" approach is not such a bad thing, if it helps one successfully cope with a difficult world. But that approach doesn't work for me – as anyone who has read this book will plainly see.

Some readers may find a small detail to pick apart. Others may take a hard look at the evidence and still not be swayed, happy to stick with the "lone gunman/magic bullet" theory until the day they die. Of course, I respect readers' right to their opinion, and in making my remarkable story public, I only hope the readers will return the favor.

Nothing in this book is meant to humiliate or humble anyone. This document is merely a record of what happened during my investigation. It is not meant to be offensive – although sometimes history and events by their very nature do offend.

The best outcome I can think of is that this book will encourage people to do two things. First, to think about the assassination of John F. Kennedy and its aftermath. Second, to keep a close and watchful eye on current events – to question and hold accountable the government that is in place to serve us.

APPENDIX

DOCUMENTS

Attached are some documents that are referred in the preceding pages. I have selected the most meaningful and, I hope, the most interesting.

The first set of documents is an FBI report that summarizes Soviet reaction to the Kennedy assassination. You will note on page that the KGB claimed to have evidence that President Lyndon Johnson had a hand in Kennedy's death.

The next documents give some information about my search for information related to Mike Hall.

Finally, I have included the letter regarding the untimely death of Mr. Wallace Engle, former employee of Lyndon Johnson.

TOP SECRET

1 - Mr. DeLoach
1 - Mr. Wick
1 - Mr. Gale
1 - Mr. Sullivan
1 - Mr. Branigan
1 - Mr. Lenihan

December 1, 1966

REC 17

ST-110

REACTION OF SOVIET AND
COMMUNIST PARTY OFFICIALS
TO THE ASSASSINATION OF
PRESIDENT JOHN F. KENNEDY

A source who has furnished reliable information
in the past and who was in Russia on the date of the
assassination of the late President John F. Kennedy advised
on December 4, 1963, that the news of the assassination of
President Kennedy was flashed to the Soviet people almost
immediately after its occurrence. It was greeted by great
shock and consternation and church bells were tolled in the
memory of President Kennedy.

According to our source, officials of the Communist
Party of the Soviet Union believed there was some well-
organized conspiracy on the part of the "ultraright" in the
United States to effect a "coup." They seemed convinced that
the assassination was not the deed of one man, but that it
arose out of a carefully planned campaign in which several
people played a part. They felt that those elements interested
in utilizing the assassination and playing on anticommunist
sentiments in the United States would then utilize this act
to stop negotiations with the Soviet Union, attack Cuba and
thereafter spread the war. As a result of these feelings,
the Soviet Union immediately went into a state of national
alert.

Our source further stated that Soviet officials
were fearful that without leadership, some irresponsible
general in the United States might launch a missile at the
Soviet Union. It was the further opinion of the Soviet
officials that only maniacs would think that the "left"
forces in the United States, as represented by the Communist
Party, USA, would assassinate President Kennedy, especially
in view of the abuse the Communist Party, USA, has taken
from the "ultraleft" as a result of its support of the
peaceful coexistence and disarmament policies of the Kennedy
administration.

62-109060

REL:kas
(8)

SECRET

Delivered to Mildred Stegall SEE NOTE PAGE 7.

MAIL ROOM ☐ TELETYPE UNIT ☐ on 12-2-66

SECRET

REACTION OF SOVIET AND COMMUNIST
PARTY OFFICIALS TO THE ASSASSINATION
OF PRESIDENT JOHN F. KENNEDY

According to our source, Soviet officials claimed
that Lee Harvey Oswald had no connection whatsoever with
the Soviet Union. They described him as a neurotic maniac
who was disloyal to his own country and everything else.
They noted that Oswald never belonged to any organization
in the Soviet Union and was never given Soviet citizenship.
(CG 5824-S*)

A second source who has furnished reliable information in the past advised on November 27, 1963, that
Nikolai T. Fedorenko, the Permanent Representative to the
Soviet Mission to the United Nations, held a brief meeting
with all diplomatic personnel employed at the Soviet Mission
on November 23, 1963. During this meeting, Fedorenko related
for the benefit of all present the news of the assassination
of President John F. Kennedy and stated that Kennedy's death
was very much regretted by the Soviet Union and had caused
considerable shock in Soviet Government circles. Fedorenko
stated that the Soviet Union would have preferred to have
had President Kennedy at the helm of the American Government.
He added that President Kennedy had, to some degree, a
mutual understanding with the Soviet Union, and had tried
seriously to improve relations between the United States
and Russia. Fedorenko also added that little or nothing
was known by the Soviet Government concerning President Lyndon
Johnson and, as a result, the Soviet Government did not know
what policies President Johnson would follow in the future
regarding the Soviet Union.

According to our source, Colonel Boris Ivanov,
Chief of the Soviet Committee for State Security (KGB)
Residency in New York City, held a meeting of KGB personnel
on the morning of November 25, 1963. Ivanov informed those
present that President Kennedy's death had posed a problem
for the KGB and stated that it was necessary for all KGB
employees to lend their efforts to solving the problem.

According to our source, Ivanov stated that it was
his personal feeling that the assassination of President
Kennedy had been planned by an organized group rather than
being the act of one individual assassin. Ivanov stated
that it was therefore necessary that the KGB ascertain with
the greatest possible speed the true story surrounding
President Kennedy's assassination. Ivanov stated that the
KGB was interested in knowing all the factors and all of
the possible groups which might have worked behind the scenes
to organize and plan this assassination.

SECRET
- 2 -

TOP SECRET

REACTION OF SOVIET AND COMMUNIST
PARTY OFFICIALS TO THE ASSASSINATION
OF PRESIDENT JOHN F. KENNEDY

Our source added that Ivanov also emphasized that
it was of extreme importance to the Soviet Government to
determine precisely what kind of a man the new President
Lyndon Johnson would be. Ivanov said that President Johnson
was practically an unknown to the Soviet Government and,
accordingly, the KGB had issued instructions to all of its
agents to immediately obtain all data available concerning
the incumbent President. Ivanov said that it would be
necessary for KGB personnel to gather and correlate all
information concerning President Johnson, including his
background, his past working experience and record in
Congress, his present attitude toward the Soviet Union, and
particularly all information which might have bearing upon
the future foreign policy line he would follow. (NY 3653-S*)

On September 16, 1965, this same source reported
that the KGB Residency in New York City received instructions
approximately September 16, 1965, from KGB headquarters in
Moscow to develop all possible information concerning
President Lyndon B. Johnson's character, background, personal
friends, family, and from which quarters he derives his
support in his position as President of the United States.
Our source added that in the instructions from Moscow, it
was indicated that "now" the KGB was in possession of data
purporting to indicate President Johnson was responsible for
the assassination of the late President John F. Kennedy.
KGB headquarters indicated that in view of this information,
it was necessary for the Soviet Government to know the
existing personal relationship between President Johnson
and the Kennedy family, particularly that between President
Johnson and Robert and "Ted" Kennedy.

On March 3, 1964, Yuri I. Nosenko, Soviet defector
whose bona fides has not been established, advised that he
was handling Soviet Committee for State Security (KGB)
investigations of tourists from the United States at the
time Lee Harvey Oswald visited Russia in 1959, and conse-
quently was fully cognizant of the Lee Harvey Oswald case.

According to Nosenko, Oswald came to the attention
of the KGB when he expressed a wish to defect to the Union
of Soviet Socialist Republics shortly after his arrival in
Russia. However, the KGB, after inquiry, decided he was
mentally unstable and informed him he had to return to the
United States upon completion of his visit. Thereafter,
when Oswald missed a sight-seeing tour he was to take, his
hotel room was forced open and he was found with one of his
wrists badly cut.

TOP SECRET

- 3 -

REACTION OF SOVIET AND COMMUNIST
PARTY OFFICIALS TO THE ASSASSINATION
OF PRESIDENT JOHN F. KENNEDY

Nosenko added that Oswald was hospitalized and
thereafter was allowed to remain in Russia, apparently
through the efforts of the Ministry of Foreign Affairs and
the Red Cross. Oswald again came to the attention of the
KGB when he attempted to re-enter the Soviet Union by placing
a request with the Soviet Embassy in Mexico, after his return
to the United States. Nosenko stated that the KGB recommended
against allowing Oswald to re-enter the Soviet Union. According to Nosenko, Oswald's case was a routine one in which the
KGB had no interest until he assassinated President Kennedy.
He was not approached or recruited for espionage by the KGB
nor was his wife, Marina. Nosenko said Marina was regarded
as a woman who possessed little intelligence and he added
that she had once been a member of the Communist Party but
had been dropped for failure over a long period of time to
pay her dues.

It was the opinion of Nosenko that President
Kennedy was held in high esteem by the Soviet Government
and that President Kennedy had been evaluated by the Soviet
Government as a person interested in maintaining peace.
According to Nosenko, following the assassination, Soviet
guards were removed from around the American Embassy in
Moscow and the Soviet people were permitted without inter-
ference to visit the American Embassy to express their
condolences. Nosenko added that the KGB provided approximately 20 men who spoke the English language to handle duties
in the immediate vicinity of the American Embassy in Moscow
at that time to insure that no disrespect was shown during
this period.

Following the assassination of President Kennedy,
Anatoli Dobrynin, Soviet Ambassador to the United States,
turned over to the Secretary of State a file alleged to be
the complete consular file on Lee H. and Marina Oswald
maintained in the Soviet Embassy, Washington, D. C.
Subsequently, the Soviet Government made available to the
United States Government the hospitalization record of
Lee Harvey Oswald during his hospitalization in the
Soviet Union. This record corroborated data previously
received indicating Oswald had attempted to commit suicide
in the Soviet Union.

Reaction of Communist Party officials to the
assassination of President Kennedy and to the investigation

SECRET

- 4

REACTION OF SOVIET AND COMMUNIST
PARTY OFFICIALS TO THE ASSASSINATION
OF PRESIDENT JOHN F. KENNEDY

conducted by the Warren Commission concerning such assassination closely follows the Soviet party line. On December 4,
1963, Gus Hall, General Secretary, Communist Party, USA,
informed one of our sources who has furnished reliable information in the past that the assassination followed a pattern
which clearly indicated it could have been done by no one
other than the "ultraright" and that Hall feels that Oswald
was killed by the "ultraright" in order to prevent him from
talking. Hall indicated to our source that he planned to
contact Soviet officials to determine if they planned to
interview Marina Oswald and, if so, he planned to ask the
Soviets to question Marina whether Lee Harvey Oswald had
any connections with the "ultraright," had any relations
with the Federal Bureau of Investigation, or had any
relations or contacts with Jack Ruby.(S)(u)

Hall also told our source that he felt the Soviets
are too lax in allowing "all kinds of persons to go to
Moscow." Hall expressed his opinion that at the time Oswald
went to Moscow, he was operating for the Federal Bureau of
Investigation. Hall further stated that Oswald "could have
been a nut, too.(X)(NY 694-S*)(X)(u)
(u)

The position of the Communist Party, USA, toward
the Warren Commission Report was clearly set forth in the
October 11, 1964, issue of "The Worker," an East Coast
communist newspaper. In an article captioned "Warren Report
Brushes Off Ultra-Rightist Conspiracy," it was stated that
the Warren Report gives comparatively very little space to
the material that came before it indicating that a
"Right-wing conspiracy" was in the making and that Oswald
was a "Left-painted" undercover instrument of such forces
or of a Government agency. The article further stated that
even the limited material which the Warren Commission has
put into the record on the Rightist conspiracy that was in
progress is an important contribution and provides a basis
for further investigation. U (

No information has been developed indicating any
of the so-called communist "splinter groups" such as the
Progressive Labor Party, Socialist Workers Party or the
Workers World Party, have planned or instituted any con-
certed effort or drive to discredit or attack the Warren
Commission. Official publications of these organizations
have from time to time contained isolated articles which
have been critical of the Warren Commission. For example,

SECRET
- 5 -

REACTION OF SOVIET AND COMMUNIST
PARTY OFFICIALS TO THE ASSASSINATION
OF PRESIDENT JOHN F. KENNEDY

"Progressive Labor," the official publication of the
Progressive Labor Party, issued a Special Supplement dated
November 27, 1963, which contained an article which attempted
to raise doubts as to whether Lee Harvey Oswald actually
killed President Kennedy. The article also attempted to
establish that Oswald possibly had been "framed." The
December, 1963, issue of this same magazine contained an
article which further attempted to establish that Oswald
had been "framed" and that the Warren Commission did not
make a thorough investigation of the assassination.

       The Soviet press, from time to time, since the
assassination of President Kennedy, has carried articles
attacking the conclusions of the Warren Commission.
Immediately following the publication of the Warren Commission
Report on September 24, 1964, the Soviet newspaper "Pravda"
carried an article in its September 28, 1964, edition
summarizing the findings of the Warren Commission. In this
article, the Soviet author stated that the Warren Commission
Report did not dispel all doubts and suspicions about the
"crime of the century." The article also noted that
"not everything mysterious has become public" and pointed
out that at the beginning of the work of the Warren Commission,
Mr. Warren declared that some facts connected with the
assassination of President Kennedy may not be revealed in
the lifetime of this generation.

       In an article in the Soviet newspaper "Investia"
for September 21, 1965, Soviet reporter V. Nerin criticized
the Warren Commission investigation and the conclusions of
the Warren Commission. The author also summarized the
allegations of a number of American and European authors
who have written books critical of the Warren Commission
Report and concluded that the assassination in Dallas has
many riddles to offer and that the mystery remains a mystery.

       In September, 1966, the Soviet publication
"New Times" published excerpts of book reviews by American
journalist Professor Richard Popkin. Among the excerpts
pointed out were comments made by Professor Popkin concerning
the books "Whitewash" by Harold Weisberg and "Inquest" by
Edward J. Epstein. The Soviet publication points out that
it is the conclusion of Professor Popkin that the Kennedy
assassination was the outcome of a carefully laid plot in
which influential quarters were implicated.

SECRET

- 8 -

94

REACTION OF SOVIET AND COMMUNIST
PARTY OFFICIALS TO THE ASSASSINATION
OF PRESIDENT JOHN F. KENNEDY

NOTE: Classified "Top Secret" because this communication
contains information from several highly sensitive sources,
the disclosure of which would result in exceptionally grave
damage to the United States.

        See cover memorandum Branigan to Sullivan, dated
12/1/66, captioned as above, prepared by REL:cls.

- 7 -

Jim Koepke
█████████ , Mn. █████

612-347-5798/884-4372

September 11, 1995

Department of the Treasury
Bureau of Alcohol, Tobacco and Firearms
Washington, D.C.   20226

Attn: Ms. Joyce A. Thomas

Dear Ms. Thomas:

I am appealing the decision of "no records response" which
is stated in your letter of Sept. 1, 1995.

The reason why I believe an adequate search was not conducted
is because I was told by ATF Agent ██████████ on May 31,
1995, that records DID exist, and that he had possession of
them. ██████████ is officed in St. Paul, Mn.

Please let me know asap what further action will be taken.

Thank you.

                                        Jim Koepke

                                        612▬▬▬▬▬

                                        December 5, 1995

The Honorable Congressman Jim Ramstad
8120 Penn Ave. S.
Bloomington, Mn.   55431

Dear Congressman Ramstad:

Could you provide some assistance with a problem I have with
the Alcohol, Tobacco and Firearms Bureau?

I was told, in May of 1995, by ATF agent ▬▬ ▬▬▬▬, who
works in the St. Paul office of the ATF, that he was in
possession of a document which referenced retired ATF Bureau
Chief Mike Hall. I asked ▬▬ ▬▬▬▬ in August of 1995 if
he would give me a copy of that document. ▬▬▬▬
refused, then told me he wasn't sure he still had it.

Since then, I have filed a Freedom of Information Act (FOIA)
with the ATF. My request has been denied on the basis that
no such document exists.

What is troubling to me is that no one in the ATF will
address the question -- what happened to the document?   The
ATF will only say that they do not have the document.

I recently sent a letter to the ATF which addressed my
concerns and they replied that they are not required to
answer my questions. Further, their latest letter appears to
make an insinuation which I take is meant to be an insult.

The most sense I can make of this is that the ATF agent who
had the document decided to destroy it. I expect this act
was done to protect his career, and that no malice was
involved.

Is it possible that someone can assist me with getting some
answers? If the document still exists, I would like to get a
copy of it. If the document has been destroyed, I would like
to know why. My assumption is that destruction of a document
which was requested under the FOIA would be an illegal act.

Thank you.

Sincerely,

Jim Koepke

RAMSTAD
DISTRICT, MINNESOTA

WAYS AND MEANS
COMMITTEE

TRADE SUBCOMMITTEE

OVERSIGHT SUBCOMMITTEE

WASHINGTON OFFICE:
103 CANNON HOUSE OFFICE BUILDING
WASHINGTON, DC 20515
(202) 225-2871

DISTRICT OFFICE
8120 PENN AVENUE SOUTH, #152
BLOOMINGTON, MN 55431
(612) 881-4600

Congress of the United States
House of Representatives
Washington, DC 20515-2303

February 12, 1996

Jim Koepke

Dear Jim:

I have received a letter from the the Bureau of Alcohol, Tobacco and Firearms in response to the inquiry I made on your behalf.

For your convenience, I am enclosing a copy of that letter. I sincerely regret the response is not more favorable.

If you have additional questions after reading the response, please call my staff person, Heather Renner.

If there is any other way I can be helpful, please don't hesitate to contact me.

Sincerely,

JIM RAMSTAD
Member of Congress

JR:hr

Enclosure

09/07/95 THU 14:42 FAX 202 724 0457   ARRB   ⓐ002

Assassination Records Review Board
600 E Street NW · 2nd Floor · Washington, DC 20530
(202) 724-0088 · Fax: (202) 724-0457

September 7, 1995

Mr.

Dear Mr. Koepke:

This is in response to the letter which you faxed to me on September 6, 1995.

I was not aware of Mr. Hall's death and regret the news. The Review Board had not contacted him and there was limited access within the office to this information.

Thank you for writing again. Please advise me if you have any additional comments, questions or information.

Sincerely,

Thomas E. Samoluk, Esq.
Associate Director for Communications

JIM KOEPKE

Jim Koepke

~~████████████~~

~~████████~~

September 21, 2000

Ms. Kathryn I. Dyer, Information and Privacy Coordinator
Central Intelligence Agency
Washington, D.C. 20505

Reference: F-1998-01100

Dear Ms. Dyer:

Thank you for your letter of 9/5/00. I do appeal the finding of "no records" concerning Mike Hall (Michael Lewis Hall), retired Federal agent.

The basis for my appeal is because Mr. Gaeton Fonzi, former investigator for the House Select Committee on Assassinations states in his book (The Last Investigation) that Mr. Hall performed a job for the Central Intelligence Agency. In his book, on page 235, Mr. Fonzi references an unnamed Federal agent. I have enclosed a copy of a letter from Mr. Fonzi that confirms the agent was, indeed, Mike Hall.

Given the above information, it appears that someone from a Federal agency asked Mr. Hall during the Spring/Summer of 1978 to do some work for them. There is no proof that it was the CIA, but Mr. Fonzi is a credible, respected investigator, and he believes it may well have been. I have enclosed copies a few pages of Mr. Fonzi's book.

Another reason for my appeal is not so well documented. The fact is, that Mr. Hall stated privately that he did do an occasional favor for the CIA. Mr. Hall further stated that some of the CIA people he worked for had knowledge of and possibly personal involvement in the assassination of President Kennedy. Given Mr. Hall's background as a Federal agent, I took this to be a serious allegation. I contacted the Assassination Records Review Board and asked them to depose Mr. Hall. They immediately assigned an investigator to interview Mr. Hall. Approximately one week later, before they could talk to Mr. Hall, he died unexpectedly. I view this death of a 54 year old man, in reportedly excellent health as suspicious. I have spoken with good friends of Mr. Hall. They find his sudden death, apparently of a heart attack, quite unbelievable.

Thank you for your consideration of my appeal.

Sincerely,

Jim Koepke

March 23, 1996

Dear Jim;

Thanks for your welcoming letter and sample Newsletter. I had mentioned that I was privy to an incident that could possibly be related, directly or peripherally, to the assassination. So, here is my story:

In the early '60s, while working in Sacramento at the Aerojet-General Corp., I met and became friends with Wallace Engle. He had previously served as an Aide to Senator Lyndon Johnson. Wally was single and we often met at his house to play chess in the evening. He had a great deal of memorabilia relating to his years serving LBJ, including testimonials and photos. It was obvious that he was quite close the senator, and that the senator thought quite highly of him.

On several occasions I tried to get Wally to open up about his experiences, but the most I ever got was that he could "curl my hair" if he chose to!

I was transferred to an east coast facility and lost contact with Wally; however, through mutual friends I learned that he had married and was leading a normal and productive life. He was certainly well thought of at Aerojet, where he served as Aide to the solid-rocket division manager.

After LBJ became president, he toured Aerojet plant and while there made a point of having Wally ride in the motorcade with him. This was well documented in the plant "house-organ".

The next I heard of Wally was a newspaper clipping sent to me describing his "suicide"! (Copy enclosed). I, and other mutual friends, were shocked. All indications were that this was a senseless, incongruous act. All outward appearances were of a man happily married and successful in his work.

I wish now that I had taken action to learn more about this matter...but I was 3000 miles away and wrapped up in my affairs. At one time I had another newspaper article, from a small local paper quoting the sheriff's deputy as saying he considered the death highly suspicious and deserving further investigation. To my knowledge, no follow-up action was ever taken. Perhaps at the time it would have been fruitful to have interviewed his widow, the deputy, the reporters and even the clerk who sold Wally the gun.

JIM KOEPKE

```
                                                        Date : 08/13/96
                                                        Page : 1
                          JFK ASSASSINATION SYSTEM
                           IDENTIFICATION FORM
---------------------------------------------------------------------
                          AGENCY INFORMATION

                 AGENCY : FBI
          RECORD NUMBER : 124-10144-10086
         RECORDS SERIES : HQ
    AGENCY FILE NUMBER : 62-109060-4321
---------------------------------------------------------------------
                         DOCUMENT INFORMATION

             ORIGINATOR : FBI
                   FROM : DIRECTOR, FBI
                     TO :
                  TITLE :
                   DATE : 12/01/66
                  PAGES : 7
               SUBJECTS : JFK, REACTION TO ASSA, CP, SOVIET CITIZENS, OFFICIALS,
                          LHO, RP, KGB

          DOCUMENT TYPE : PAPER, TEXTUAL DOCUMENT
         CLASSIFICATION : UNCLASSIFIED
           RESTRICTIONS : OPEN IN FULL
         CURRENT STATUS : OPEN
    DATE OF LAST REVIEW : 08/13/96
       OPENING CRITERIA :
               COMMENTS :
```

BIBLIOGRAPHY

Axelrod, A. & Phillips, C. (1992). *What Every American Should Know About American History: 200 Events That Shaped the Nation.* Holbrook, MA: Adams Media Corporation.

Barrett, W.P. & Lucas, C. (1984, March 25). "Sources: Estes Wouldn't Testify on JFK Assassination." *Dallas Times Herald.* P. unknown.

Belin, D. (1988). *Full Disclosure.* New York: Scribner.

Belzer, R. (2000). *UFO's, JFK, & Elvis: Conspiracies you don't have to be crazy to believe.* New York: Ballantine Books.

Breo, D.L. (May 27, 1992). JFK's death – the plain truth from the MDs who did the autopsy and JFK's death, part II – Dallas MDs recall their memories. *JAMA, The Journal of the American Medical Association.*

Crenshaw, C. (1992). JFK – Conspiracy of Silence. New York: Signet.

Davis, J. (1989). *Mafia Kingfish: Carlos Marcello and the Assassination of John F. Kennedy.* New York: Signet / New American Library.

"Former LBJ Aide Is Apparent Suicide." (1966, December 2). *The Sacramento Bee*, p. D4.

Fonzi, G. (1993). *The Last Investigation.* New York: Thunder's Mouth Press.

Geewax, M. (1993, September 2). Put to rest those JFK conspiracy myths. *Minneapolis Star Tribune. p.19A.*

Gold, G.,editor. (1974). *The White House Transcripts*. New York: Bantam Books.

Goldberg, B. (2002). *Bias: a CBS Insider Exposes How the Media Distort the News.* Washington D.C: Regnery Publishing, Inc.

Groden, R.J. & Livingstone, H.E. (1989). *High Treason.* New York: Berkley Books.

Haldeman, H.R. (1978). *The Ends of Power.* New York: Time Books.

Hanners, D. (1984, March 23). Billie Sol links LBJ to murder. *The Dallas Morning News.* p. 4.

Lane, M. (1992). *Plausible denial.* New York: Thunder's Mouth Press.

Lane, M. (1992). *Rush to Judgement.* New York: Thunder's Mouth Press.

Lynch, D. of the Albany Times Union. (1995, March 30). Stone, audience don't bother with pesky facts. *Minneapolis Star Tribune.* p.17A.

Posner, G. (1994). *Case Closed.* New York: Anchor.

Powers, T. (1979). *The Man Who Kept the Secrets: Richard Helms and the CIA.* New York: Pocket Books.

Prouty, L.F. (1992). *JFK: the CIA, Vietnam, and the Plot to Assassinate John F. Kennedy.* New York: Carol.

"Purported letter from Jack Ruby implicates LBJ." (1995, April 15). *Minneapolis Star Tribune.* p.4A.

"Report shows discrepancies in brain exams in JFK's autopsy." (1998, November 10). *Washington Post*, reprinted in the *Minneapolis Star Tribune*, p.A13.

Scheim, D. (1989). *Contract on America: The Mafia Murder of President John F. Kennedy.* New York: Zebra Books/ Kensington Publishing Corp.

Stone, O. (1991 Film). *JFK.*

Thomas, E. (1993, November 22). The real cover-up. *Newsweek.* p.66.

United States. (1964). Warren Commission. *Report of the Warren Commission on the Assassination of President Kennedy*. New York: Bantam Books.

Wecht, C. (1994). *Cause of Death: The Shocking True Stories Behind the Headlines – a forensic expert speaks out on JFK, RFK, Elvis, Chappaquiddick, and other controversial cases*. New York: Onyx/ Penguin Books.

Printed in the United States
22476LVS00001B/167

9 781413 713961